# THE PRICE OF VALOR

# THE PRICE OF
# VALOR

## THE LIFE OF AUDIE MURPHY, AMERICA'S MOST DECORATED HERO OF WORLD WAR II

# DAVID A. SMITH

REGNERY
HISTORY

Regnery History™ is a trademark of Salem Communications Holding Corporation; Regnery® is a registered trademark of Salem Communications Holding Corporation

Library of Congress Cataloging-in-Publication Data

Smith, David A., 1966-
    The price of valor : the life of Audie Murphy / David A. Smith.
        pages cm
    ISBN 978-1-62157-317-3
    1.  Murphy, Audie, 1924-1971. 2.  United States. Army--Biography. 3.  World War, 1939-1945--Campaigns--Western Front. 4.  Medal of Honor--Biography. 5.  Soldiers--United States--Biography. 6.  Motion picture actors and actresses--United States--Biography. I. Title.
    U53.M87S65 2015
    940.54'1273092--dc23
    [B]

                                    2015005216

Published in the United States by
Regnery History
An imprint of Regnery Publishing
A Division of Salem Media Group
300 New Jersey Ave NW
Washington, DC 20001
www.RegneryHistory.com

Manufactured in the United States of America

10 9 8 7 6 5 4 3 2 1

Books are available in quantity for promotional or premium use. For information on discounts and terms, please visit our website: www.Regnery.com.

Distributed to the trade by
Perseus Distribution
250 West 57th Street
New York, NY 10107

*In Memory of*
*My Friend and Colleague*
*Dan Greene*

# CONTENTS

# INTRODUCTION

H is grave is marked by a standard Arlington Cemetery tombstone of white marble, just like the hundreds of thousands of others. It stands at the end of a row, shaded by the branches of a massive Willow Oak tree, beside the road that passes north of the amphitheater near the Tomb of the Unknowns. Groundskeepers built a flagstone walkway around the tree to accommodate the steady trickle of visitors. Each day, small groups of people drift over, some of them clutching a map from the visitor center, obviously searching for the grave. They pause and a few take off their hats. They speak to each other in hushed tones. Some obviously know more about the record of achievement that is abbreviated on the front of the stone than do others. "The Medal of Honor," one man says softly to his companion. "They don't just give those away."

Seen from afar, among the orderly ranks and files of headstones this one is indistinguishable from all the others. Approaching closer, one may notice a small American flag pushed into the soft ground beside it. Its story of honor and heroism is only hinted at by the letters inscribed on the gravestone.

Audie L. Murphy occupies a distinct place in the roster of famous Americans. During his short, troubled life, he served as an American archetype in at least two ways. First and foremost, he was a soldier and decorated war hero—the most decorated American soldier of the Second World War. His actions in World War II were of the sort from which chroniclers, balladeers, and poets since the days of the ancient Greeks have composed legends. He was the man charging headlong into fortified enemy positions, holding his own against an onslaught of enemy soldiers, defying the odds. Always brave. Always valorous. Always alone.

Second, Audie Murphy was a movie star. He made nearly fifty movies in a career that spanned twenty-three years—ten times as long as the war experience that made him famous—and during his peak of popularity received more fan mail than almost any other actor. The quality of the movies he made varied widely as he took on westerns, war movies, and "serious" contemporary scripts. Some directors with whom he worked coaxed stirring, praiseworthy performances from him that seemed to portend a hopeful career. In other films, critics would pointedly and acidulously note that he seemed lost, detached, or simply going through the motions: an actor distracted, a man unable to engage.

Murphy was not alone in being a movie star who served in the war. Other leading men like Clark Gable and Jimmy Stewart did so, although neither was as decorated as Murphy himself would be. Unlike them or, say, baseball player Ted Williams, Audie Murphy was not an established star celebrity who went off to war, but instead a poor boy from Texas who volunteered for the Army in 1942, a year *before* his eighteenth birthday. He endured some of the toughest sustained infantry combat in the European Theater. Few people beyond his division had heard his name when he became the most decorated soldier of the war and was suddenly hailed as a hero.

In the summer of 1945, his face, impossibly young and fresh, appeared on the cover of *Life* magazine. *Life* at the time was the supreme arbiter of all things American, the herald and billboard of the "American Century," and to appear on its cover was to embody all that the country wanted to think of itself. More than anyone else, Murphy became the very incarnation of the average American who went to war, performed valorous and selfless deeds, and then came home to resume his life—except that in Murphy's case, he did not return to the poor, small town, rural Texas that he knew but to a life in Hollywood and of celebrity.

"War makes strange giant creatures out of us little routine men who inhabit the earth," said journalist Ernie Pyle, who reported the news from the Italian front while Audie Murphy was fighting there. When the war was done, Murphy was a national hero, and to his embarrassment and obvious ill-ease he was treated like a dignitary, given parades, and made to give speeches. Hardly before the shock of being home had worn off, he found himself summoned to Hollywood by one of the biggest stars in the movie business.[1]

There were, of course, other Congressional Medal of Honor winners and many other heroes in the war, but few became permanent celebrities, let alone of the Hollywood sort; and in Audie Murphy the tension between the real-life heroism he performed on the battlefield and the celebrity that was awarded him afterward was almost always evident.

Jack Valenti, a fellow Texan and veteran, journalist, and longtime president of the Motion Picture Association of America, wrote that "the important fact, the significance of Audie Murphy's valor, is that he was a simple, ordinary youngster, with no indications or outcroppings to show the stern courage within him that was shortly to burn as bright as the glint of the sun."[2]

Indeed, one of the complexities of Audie Murphy's story is that he did seem on the surface so thoroughly simple and ordinary. It was a central ingredient, even, of his cultural image. What made him so appealing, however, was not his being *average* but rather his being *emblematic*—the ideal of "everyday American" virtue, an embodiment of Norman Rockwell America. He was how the country wanted to think of itself.

Yet, lurking below the Norman Rockwell–like image of Audie Murphy was what we now call "Post-Traumatic Stress Disorder," from which he so clearly and devastatingly suffered. During World War II it was called "battle fatigue" and in the war before that "shell shock." Whatever the label, it plagued him for the rest of his life after the war. It was a condition which at the time was little understood, and for the treatment of which there was almost no help available. He was aware of how it affected him and sometimes gave way to bitterness about it.

Killing, psychologists say, is "the single most pervasive, traumatic experience of war." Second to this is the emotional distress experienced by observing violence and the death of friends and comrades. Murphy had done more than his fair share of killing and seeing others killed. Despite an appealingly fresh-faced and youthful appearance that stayed with him well into his adult years, his wartime trauma left him scarred. There was always a profound melancholy just under his surface along with a fatalism that was completely at odds with his image. The tension made him an interesting actor, but it came at a high cost.[3]

"Before the war, I'd get excited and enthused about a lot of things," he once admitted to film director John Huston, "but not any more." Murphy often appeared withdrawn and depressed, unable to focus too long on any one task. Overwhelmed by pessimism, he was subject to hair-raising bouts of temper. He was tormented by nightmares. Within a week of flying home he was reliving the war in his dreams. He would wake up yelling for his buddies who had died in his arms. He slept with the light on, and then resorted to sleeping pills. Military historian Max Hastings described Audie Murphy as "a psychological mess of epic proportions."[4]

Some of Murphy's torments also had their roots in his childhood, which was marked by profound insecurities. Murphy came of age during the Great Depression and the uncertainty of those years left their mark on him. In his acclaimed book *The Greatest Generation*, journalist Tom Brokaw noted that children like Audie Murphy "watched their parents lose their businesses, their farms, their jobs, their hopes. They had learned to accept a future that played out one day at a time." Murphy never looked far into the future; the present was always enough of a challenge. His father's periodic absences and the strain they put on his mother also affected him deeply. He was both fiercely proud and remarkably withdrawn. Even when he was a young boy, adults who knew him sensed his pride, his sensitivity, and his anger.[5]

But it was Murphy's war trauma that shaped his adult life more than anything else, and his responses to the distinctive stresses of war are not unique. A friend of mine who teaches at the U.S. Army Command and General Staff College once told me that there were certain clips from movies he refused to show to any of his classes in which there were veterans. The images and, even more, the sounds of combat, he said, could trigger terrible and unpredictable reactions. Given this, the more one knows about Audie Murphy's story the more difficult it is to watch *To Hell and Back*, the 1955 film version of his life based on his memoir in which he starred as himself. Not only was a fragile and lonely soul made to relive the pain of his mother's death, but amid Hollywood-choreographed explosions and gunfire he was made to relive the deaths of his closest companions as well.

In the 1959 movie *No Name on the Bullet*, a psychological drama in the form of a western, Murphy plays a hired killer named John Gant who has grown numb from his line of work, and speaks of death with cold detachment. In this movie, as in so many others he made, Murphy's character is low-key, a man of few words, a distant look in his eyes; a man who has been drained by his experiences.

"I can't make my mind accept that Gant is the vicious killer I know him to be," says the town doctor at one point. "I've played chess with him. I've talked with him. I found myself liking him." Similarly, it might be hard to recognize not only the war hero but the tormented veteran in the small, quiet young man who stepped off the Army transport plane returning home to instant fame. "A man can't escape his past," another character remarks of John Gant. That certainly became true for Audie Murphy.

The tree that shades Murphy's tombstone in Arlington Cemetery, and on hot summer days provides a welcome relief to those who come to find his final resting place and pay their respects, also hints at the shadow the war cast over his life. His story is one of triumph, trauma, and ultimately tragedy. He was a man who, without ever intending to be, had to live out his life as the most decorated soldier of World War II and one of the most celebrated heroes in American history.

# CHAPTER ONE

# A CHILD OF THE DEPRESSION

S hadows from the tree lines were just beginning to stretch out across the dry, dusty cotton fields on the evening of June 20, 1925, when the telephone rang. As one of the few physicians in northern Hunt County, Texas, a rural area fifty miles northeast of Dallas, Doc Pearson was accustomed to his phone ringing at all hours. This time it was interrupting his dinner. On the other end of the line was Emmett Murphy, a poor tenant farmer calling from the home of the man on whose land he was currently working. His wife was going into labor and needed the doctor to come at once.[1]

It didn't take long for the doctor to drive the bumpy white gravel roads that snaked around and through the fields to the Murphys' small, four-room clapboard cabin. When he arrived, he found two women neighbors attending to Josie Murphy inside. Emmett and the Murphys' three children waited anxiously outside in the front yard. The Murphys knew how fragile life could be. In 1919, their ten-month-old daughter

Virginia Oneta had died; in 1920, their four-year-old son Vernon had died of pneumonia, a complication from influenza; and that same year a son they had planned to name J. W. was stillborn. At about 7:00 p.m., the doctor stepped onto the porch and congratulated Murphy on the birth of an apparently healthy son.

Previously, the Murphys had made a habit of naming their children prior to birth, but by the time their seventh arrived they were perhaps wary. Eventually the family settled on the first name of "Audie," after one of their neighbors whose wife had helped Josie during her pregnancy. The baby's oldest sister Corinne suggested "Leon" as a middle name. It was a far cry from the grand names of Audie's paternal and maternal grandparents, George Washington Murphy and Jefferson Davis Killian.

The fanciful image of the "Roaring Twenties" had very little to do with the reality of life in rural Hunt County, Texas. Here in the Blackland Prairie, cotton was still king and there were just enough creeks and shade trees to provide cover for deer, rabbits, and squirrels. The entire population of the county was a little more than 50,000 people, about one third the size of Dallas in 1925. Greenville, the county seat, had the largest cottonseed oil mill in the South and there was big money to be made in the business, but for the families who tilled the fields, there was very little money in cotton. Fewer than one in three owned the land on which they worked, and those that didn't regularly drifted from farm to farm. Emmett Murphy was one of those always on the move, moving from the Boles farm near Kingston where Audie was born to farms near the smaller communities of Hog Eye, White Rock, and Lane.

From the time he could walk and pull weeds Audie worked in the fields alongside his father, mother, and older siblings. Sometimes an uncle or two—usually Josie's brothers Charles and William Killian whom Audie especially liked—would join them in the cotton fields.

Audie had five uncles who had served in World War I, including Charles and William, and one who came back from the war with a permanent hacking cough from being exposed to poison gas. Audie grew up hearing stories of the Great War and of what it was like to be a soldier. To him combat sounded like a tremendous adventure, far removed from the drudgery of the cotton fields. In his daydreams, the hoe became his weapon; weeds were the enemy soldiers, and Army life seemed a great alternative to living off the land.

As a child, Audie was particularly close to his sister Corinne who was fourteen years his senior and who took a large role in raising him. She put him to bed each night, singing and rocking him to sleep. Despite the family's deprivations, Corinne remembered him as "a happy child" who "laughed a great deal and when he laughed his eyes just sparkled."

Like many boys, Audie liked dogs, and they liked him. When he was about three years old, some neighbors gave him a dog named Wheeler, and the two became inseparable. But then came the first of many sudden shocks to his world: his sister Corinne left home when he was five and moved to the small town of Farmersville to live with her grandparents.

---

The run-down houses in which Audie grew up had no plumbing or electricity. Josie did the cooking on a wood burning stove, and heat came from a fireplace if there was one. The family got its milk from one cow that traveled with them from place to place. The thin walls of their homes barely kept out the weather, and Audie would always remember the "wail of wind around a shanty." In 1933 the family was evicted from their house in Lane for nonpayment of rent. "Poverty," Audie wrote, "dogged our every step."[2]

The Great Depression hit regions like Hunt County particularly hard. Cotton prices were always volatile, but after the great stock market crash in late October 1929, cotton prices took a harrowing plunge. By July 1931, they had fallen from 16 cents to 10 cents a pound; in September cotton went for a little more than 6 cents a pound; and at the beginning of October, it hit the unprecedented low of just 4.7 cents per pound. At that price, a 500-pound bale of cotton—which represented two hundred man-hours of work—would bring only $23.50. One field hand, in circumstances not unlike Emmett Murphy's, said he had made a mere 91 cents from an entire week's worth of hard work. "I can starve just as easily sitting down as I can picking cotton," he said sadly. In July 1932, most small town newspapers stopped printing the daily cotton price. It was just too depressing.[3]

In September 1931, a special session of the Texas legislature passed a bill intending to prop up cotton prices by strictly limiting the number of acres farmers could plant in the following year. Even though the Texas Supreme Court voided the law in 1932, many landowners stopped planting on their own initiative because of the low prices. In November 1933, the U.S. Congress passed a law regulating cotton production by means of gin quotas. Consequently, with fewer acres under cultivation, it became harder for families like the Murphys to find work.

After they left the community of Lane, the Murphys moved to the small town of Celeste, living for a few months in a converted boxcar before moving into a rental house—little more than a shack—on the east edge of town, two blocks off the main street. The rent was $4 a month and here the family at least had electricity—a bare bulb hanging from a cord in each room—for the first time. And, for the first time, they actually had next-door neighbors. John Cawthon was a barber in town and he and his wife Willie became close friends of the Murphys (Audie's sister Willie, born in 1933, was named after Mrs. Cawthon). The Cawthons looked out for the Murphy children and helped take care of them. Soon Audie was at their house more often than at his own. On the weekends Mr. Cawthon would sometimes give his boys money to go to Greenville and see a movie, and he always made sure to give Audie enough to go with them. Audie's favorite movies were westerns and his favorite star was Gary Cooper. He was already developing a sense of responsibility for his younger brothers and sisters, and every time he went into town, he returned with candy for them.[4]

It was while living in Celeste that nine-year-old Audie began attending school. Even though he was at least two years older than most of the other boys in first grade, he was small in stature, and even as a boy looked younger than his years. Despite his late start at education, he usually liked school and loved to read, and was a good student who made mostly A's and B's. He became particularly close with his second grade teacher and would often stay after class and help her clean the classroom. Some of his teachers would often share their lunches with him since he rarely brought a lunch of his own.

His teachers recognized Audie as sensitive, stubborn, and proud. Once, in third grade, he skipped school for two days after being spanked for a transgression. Although he hated it, all his teachers in Celeste called him "Little Pat" simply because he was of Irish descent and his father was called "Pat." He also particularly hated "Little Britches," which he was called because while he grew, his one pair of overalls did not. Audie had an ungovernable temper to go along with his pride. "At school, I had fought a great deal," he admitted. "Perhaps I was trying to level with my fists what I assumed fate had put above me." "I was a mean kid," he said.

His teachers thought better of him. Audie was "intelligent, industrious, quick to anger, but very loyal and devoted to the ones he loved," one of his teachers said. "It makes me sad to think how unhappy my 'Fighting Irishman' must have been during his lifetime, when he had such great potential to have a wonderful life."[5]

Audie grew up hunting, mostly as a way to secure meat for the dinner table. As a young boy, he could hit and kill a running rabbit with a rock. He quickly graduated from rocks to slingshots then to a .22 rifle, and with each weapon he displayed remarkable aim against rabbits, squirrels, and birds, sometimes seeing targets no one else could spot. His hearing was just as sharp as his eyesight and he could locate a squirrel in a tree just from the sound of a cracking twig. While he was tracking down a squirrel or a bird, completely focused in the moment, he was truly content. One relative later recalled that "about the only fun he ever had was hunting."

John Cawthon was an avid dove hunter, and because his own sons did not like to hunt, he took Audie with him. Once Audie disappeared over the crest of hill, and Cawthon heard multiple blasts from a shotgun. He returned to find Audie surrounded by so many doves that they exceeded the state limit. His marksmanship may seem legendary, but there was an undeniable reason for him to be a good shot. "If I missed, we didn't eat," he said. He also knew that he couldn't afford enough bullets to be a bad shot.

Audie's other ideas of fun were dangerous in the extreme. He and his friends shot beer bottles off of each other's heads and shot sticks and cigarettes out of their hands in what they called "Hunt County Roulette." It was foolhardy, but a friend remembered that "Audie had great courage and always accepted a challenge." Audie had supreme confidence in his ability to put a bullet precisely where he wanted it, and his trusting, willing friends must have shared that confidence.

———

If shooting and hunting were things that Audie Murphy did well, providing for a family was something that his father Emmett Murphy did not do well at all. Audie denied that his father was lazy but conceded that "he had a genius for not considering the future." Some of

Murphy's neighbors in Celeste were less generous, grousing that Emmett Murphy was a layabout. His house was filthy, his wife and children ill-cared for. In fact, one of Audie's sisters, who worked as a domestic helper for another family, was required by her employer to take a bath before she started work.

What was talked about less openly was that Irish "Pat," as Emmett Murphy was known, drank heavily, and sometimes spent the night sleeping off a hangover in the town jail.[6]

Nights spent in jail were not Pat's only disappearances from his family. Audie's father could abandon them for days or even weeks without warning. By the 1930s, Emmett Murphy's recurrent absences had left his family dependent on the charity of neighbors and, after 1933, the various direct relief programs of the New Deal. While they lived in Celeste, women from the Baptist and Methodist churches regularly came by the house—or the boxcar—to drop off food, clothes, and even medicine occasionally.

"Every time my old man couldn't feed the kids he had," Audie said later in life with the perspective that only time could bring, "he got himself another one." "I suppose I hated him," he admitted, "because I hate anyone who quits." He resolved that he would not be like his father.

Audie Murphy was far closer to his mother. Thirty-five when Audie was born, Josie Murphy had already given birth six times and lost three children. She was prematurely aged, and in increasingly ill health. When she was healthy, she worked in the fields alongside her husband and children, and when Emmett was gone she had to work even harder. One of Audie's first chores as a little boy was to massage her hands in the evenings after she worked in the fields all day; they were hands that also, amazingly, could play the piano, which she did at the Baptist church. It bonded them deeply together. Audie claimed his earliest memory "was wanting to do something for her. I still feel guilty that I never could."

In 1937, after four years in Celeste the family moved to work on a farm near the small town of Floyd, west of Greenville. Though he was now only thirteen, Audie stopped going to school and started working full time at whatever jobs he could find. He was a hard worker in everything he did, from selling magazine subscriptions door to door, to working on other farms, to working for a building contractor in Farmersville who paid him full wages because "he did a man's work." Though at the insistence of his mother he returned to school in Floyd for a year, finishing fifth grade, by 1939, when he was fifteen, he left home and school for good, going to work for a man named Haney Lee who owned a nearby farm.

Audie moved in with the Lee family as a hired hand, making $1.50 a day along with room and board. Like the Cawthons in Celeste, Haney Lee and his wife became something of surrogate parents for him. Mr. Lee taught him how to drive and when he was not working in the fields Audie did the dishes alongside Mrs. Lee and helped with the housework. All of Audie's early employers regarded him as a hard worker who, unlike his father, kept himself neat and clean. "He was a fanatic about cleanliness," Lee's wife remembered.

In 1940, Audie took a job in Greenville at a combination gas station and grocery store owned by Mrs. Lee's brother Snow Warren. He was now making $12 a week at a time when a farmhand could only make between $1 and $1.50 a day. Goldie Warren, Snow Warren's wife, said that Audie was "neat as a pin" when he showed up to work, and charmingly humble and shy. Like his teachers, she also saw his pride hidden just beneath the surface and described him as a "sad type person." It is not hard to see the adult Audie Murphy in that description.

Audie was ambitious too and working at a gas station was not how he envisioned his future. He approached Jake Bowen, who owned the local radio repair shop, and asked him for a job, thinking he could learn more skills and eventually make more money there. Bowen told him that the shop needed extra help, but he couldn't afford to hire anyone. Still, he invited Murphy to live with his family and learn the business. Audie accepted.

Most people who knew Audie at this time called him by his middle name, "Leon," and Bowen was among the many who liked Murphy; he saw him as "an eager beaver worker" and "an All-American boy type." Not only did he work hard, he was clean and neat, never used bad language, did not drink, and, after one ill-fated experiment with a pipe, steered clear of tobacco as well. After a while, he moved into a garage apartment with Jake Bowen's cousin Bill, who kept the books for the radio shop. He went to see an occasional movie in Greenville and spent his spare time building model airplanes that he hung from the ceiling of his room.

In 1940, Audie's father left home again, and this time he did not return. For a while after her husband disappeared Josie and the children continued to live in their house, with Corinne and other ladies who lived nearby bringing them meals and Audie sending over what little money he could from Greenville. Finally, however, when her health started to fail, she and the children moved in with Corinne and her family.

Even though she now had some help with the children, Josie's heath continued to decline. In the spring of 1941 she developed an infection in the lining of her heart. Bedridden and weak, she then came down with pneumonia in May and faded quickly. Audie hurried over from Greenville where he was working at Bowen's radio shop and stayed with the family. On the afternoon of May 23, Audie was hoeing in his sister's backyard garden when he was summoned urgently into the house. Shortly after, his mother died with Audie at her side, gently rubbing her hands as he had done so many times over the course of her hard life. She was five days short of her fiftieth birthday. Her death left a hole he would never be able to fill.

Her funeral was the next afternoon at the funeral home in Farm-ersville, officiated by the pastor of First Baptist Church and punctu-ated by the small group of mourners singing her three favorite hymns that she herself had played so many times on countless pianos in little church houses. Afterwards a modest, three-car procession winded its way to the Prairie Grove cemetery just south of Farmersville. Audie borrowed money from Jake Bowen to help pay for the simple funeral, and the funeral home allowed him to defer some of the payment he owed them. After the funeral Murphy went to Celeste to break the news to the Cawthons. He was crying on their porch when Mrs. Cawthon returned home.

Audie and his sister Corinne, who was married now and with a child of her own, followed their mother's wishes and sent their three youngest siblings to Boles Orphans Home near Greenville. He was sixteen and now an orphan himself. His future would, astonishingly, not depend on his own efforts scraping a living in Texas, but on events thousands of miles away, in the plans of the Japanese empire and the aggressive wars being waged by Nazi Germany and Fascist Italy.

# CHAPTER TWO

# FINDING A PURPOSE

W hen Audie Murphy was in school in Celeste, he told his friend Monroe Hackney that he wanted to be a soldier. The tales of combat he had heard from his uncles out in the fields stayed with him through the years, and he saw the Army as the best and most adventurous way of getting as far away as possible from the hard life that he knew.

After he buried his mother, Audie Murphy was a lost soul. He returned to Greenville, the garage apartment, his model airplanes, and his job at the radio repair shop. After the shop closed, he went back to work on the Haney's farm, also hiring himself out to a farmer who lived nearby named A. L. Springfield. He went out on dates, sometimes doubling with a friend. He continued to go to movies, and in 1941 could have indulged his love for westerns abundantly. The major studios released dozens of them. In May, Robert Taylor played the title role in *Billy the Kid*. In October, William Holden and Glenn

Ford's *Texas* was released. Along with these there were several movies starring the singing cowboys Gene Autry and Roy Rogers, and, most of all, the innumerable "B" westerns. Offerings like *Badlands of Dakota, King of the Texas Rangers, Six-Gun Gold,* and *Bad Men of Missouri* promised simple plots with lots of action.

But it was a different sort of movie that hit Audie the hardest. *Sergeant York* was released by the Warner Brothers studio in September 1941 and arrived in Greenville in October. He liked it so much that he saw it twice. His favorite actor, Gary Cooper, portrayed the true-life World War I hero who had come from a background somewhat similar to Murphy's—a poor Southern farmer who happened to be a crack shot with a rifle. In the movie, and in real life, that skill proved its worth on the battlefield, and with war again raging in Europe, it was a skill that might soon be in demand once more.

Audie and Monroe Hackney were in Greenville on a double date on Sunday, December 7, 1941, when they heard the Japanese had attacked Pearl Harbor. Congress declared war on Japan on December 8, 1941. Japan's allies Nazi Germany and Fascist Italy declared war on the United States on December 11.

"It is not a sacrifice for any man, old or young, to be in the Army or Navy of the United States. Rather it is a privilege," President Franklin Roosevelt told the nation on December 9, 1941. Enlistment stations were deluged with volunteers who wanted that privilege. Before the attack on Pearl Harbor, the Marine Corps' weekly high for recruitment had been 552 men. Now the Marines were signing up as many as 6,000 men a week. Almost 45,000 men joined the Marines in the three months following Pearl Harbor. Audie Murphy tried to enlist in the Marine Corps in 1942, declaring that he wanted to be a sniper. He was turned away: he was too young, too short, and underweight.

He kept trying, but was repeatedly turned away from recruiting stations until he successfully enlisted in the Army in June 1942.

Because Audie was only five feet, five inches tall and weighed only 112 pounds, the recruiting officer in Greenville demanded proof of his age. Audie and his sister went to a notary a few days later in Collin County (in which Farmersville was located) and filled out the requisite forms. She was also required to testify that there were no family members who depended on his support. But how old was Audie Murphy *really*? His enlistment papers state that he was born in 1924. Murphy's California driver's license from much later in his life gives his birthdate as 1925, and he occasionally admitted that he was born in 1925. His friend David McClure, who after the war helped Murphy write his combat memoir *To Hell and Back*, also said that Murphy joined the army on his seventeenth birthday. That was not the only odd thing about his enlistment papers. His mother, who had guided him in religious matters, had been a Baptist, but Murphy listed his religious denomination as Methodist. Denominations would never be very important to him.[1]

The next day Audie Murphy was formally inducted into the U.S. Army at the Federal Building in downtown Dallas, and then boarded a bus to Camp Wolters, where he would begin his basic training.

---

Camp Wolters, some fifty miles west of Fort Worth, had been established in the 1920s as a Texas National Guard base. In 1941, the U.S. Army took it over and designated it one of several Infantry Replacement Training Centers. It encompassed thousands of rambling acres about four miles east of Mineral Wells, a town that advertised itself as "the South's Greatest Health Resort." At its peak during the war, the camp housed almost 25,000 soldiers in row after row of rectangular white barracks. Its purpose was "nondivisional training," that is, to train a steady supply of unassigned replacement infantrymen that the Army would then send as needed to units already in action overseas whose numbers had been reduced by combat casualties.

Audie Murphy and the other newest members of the U.S. Army arrived at Camp Wolters on the evening of June 30. They were given a booklet explaining the training they were about to undergo. "The infantryman is primarily a foot soldier," it stressed to the apprehensive recruits. "With the various weapons of the infantry he is the heart of the Army." Murphy was issued a World War I style uniform (right down to the distinctive helmet), an army haircut, and a rifle. He was assigned to the fourth platoon of Company D of the 59th Training Battalion. He signed up for the typical serviceman's life insurance policy in the amount of $5,000, naming Corinne, technically his guardian since the death of his mother, as his beneficiary and next of kin. He thought about taking out a higher amount, but "I don't intend to get killed any way and it costs pretty high." (It was 67 cents per $1,000.) As soon as he was able, he sent a $25 payment to the funeral home in Farmersville that had extended him credit after his mother died.

Basic training lasted thirteen weeks, but early on Murphy stood out as one of the most promising soldiers in the entire battalion. Army life suited him: the rules, the responsibility, and the insistence on neatness, order, and cleanliness. While some thought the rigors of the Army harsh, they were no harder to Audie than life in the cotton fields. His fellow soldiers could see that Murphy loved the Army: the long marches, the bivouacs in the field, the weapons training—it was everything of his boyhood dreams; one of his buddies even thought that for Murphy it was like "playing cowboys and Indians." He took his training seriously but enjoyed it so much he was smiling all the time. He still looked youthful—boyish even—and something of an incongruity in the middle of bayonet and rifle drills. The First

Sergeant of the platoon took to calling him "Baby," a nickname he naturally hated.

Murphy particularly enjoyed shooting, and learned to fire the standard issue M-1 Garand rifle along with light and medium machine guns and a light mortar. He so stood out for his ability to field strip and reassemble his Springfield '03 model rifle (which he could do blindfolded) that he was chosen by the platoon Corporal to demonstrate the procedure for men who were not getting it. He earned his marksmanship badge with the rifle and the higher-rated expert badge with the bayonet.

One day during a bayonet drill he suddenly passed out. The Texas summer heat had risen well over one hundred degrees and he had just received a series of immunizations, which probably had something to do with it. He spent a couple of days in the camp hospital before rejoining his company. The episode was not serious, but it hinted at a vulnerability: Audie's health was always somewhat frail; he was prone to sickness. That vulnerability, and his small size, prompted his commanding officers to suggest he switch training tracks and become a cook or something like that. Audie refused and stuck to his intention of becoming an infantryman.

There was a beer garden near one of the post exchanges that the soldiers had christened "the 50th Battalion," and Murphy sometimes went with his buddies. In addition to beer, it sold tobacco, soft drinks, and ice cream, and had a jukebox. Because of what a friend would later characterize as "a trick stomach that rebelled against alcohol," Murphy would only order soft drinks, but he enjoyed the masculine camaraderie of the place.[2]

After thirteen weeks of basic training, he had a short break before moving on to more advanced infantry training. On leave, he returned to Farmersville, where he made a tremendous impression on people who had known him before. Audie had taken to the army "like he was born in it," said his sister. He carried himself erect and moved with a snap and a precision he never learned on the farm.

On October 13, 1942, Murphy was back at Camp Wolters ready to board a train to Maryland and the advanced infantry training base at Fort Meade, soon to be designated the main Overseas Replacement Depot for the Atlantic coast, with more than 2.5 million soldiers passing through its gates during the war. The trip from Texas took five days. As at Camp Wolters, Audie thrived at working with weapons and tackling obstacle courses.

According to one story, Murphy picked up a .22 rifle at a carnival-type shooting gallery just outside the gates of the post and proceeded to shoot out five hearts (or diamonds) on a standard playing card from thirty feet away. The gallery operator refused to pay out the $25 prize Murphy's feat merited. Murphy reported the incident to his company commander; his testimony was corroborated by a buddy who was at the shooting gallery with him. The next day the officer paid a visit to the shooting gallery proprietor and bluntly explained that the choice facing him was either to pay Private Murphy the money he owed him, or else have his gallery put on the off-limits list. The gallery owner agreed to pay but said he never wanted to see Murphy there again.

Another story recounted how Murphy was assigned to escort two prisoners convicted of violent crimes. Far bigger than Murphy, they tried to escape, but stopped when Murphy flipped the safety on his shotgun. There was something in Murphy's tone of his voice that convinced them that he meant it when he said he would shoot them both dead. It was a tone of voice that Murphy later used to convincingly portray western gunfighters in his films. It was an actual part of him; he might have been small and baby-faced, but he came by his toughness naturally.

Despite Murphy's proficiency with weapons and with every infantry task he was assigned, his superior officers looked him up and down and deemed him better suited to something else. His company commander offered to reassign him to the Post Exchange, keeping him stateside. Murphy was appalled at the idea and emphatically declined the offer. He had no desire to spend the war disbursing supplies and equipment to other men who were going off to do the real fighting.

Completing his training at Fort Meade, Murphy was transferred to Camp Kilmer in New Jersey on January 23, 1943, to be readied for overseas deployment to North Africa, although as yet no one knew exactly where they would be going. Rumors nevertheless abounded as the Navy gathered troop transport ships and destroyer escorts. Murphy was one of more than 1.3 million soldiers in more than twenty divisions who passed through sprawling Camp Kilmer during World War II. The camp was more like a small city with more than 1,100 buildings (including several movie theaters, at one of which Audie saw the movie *Casablanca*, not knowing he would soon be in that exotic city).

Had Audie Murphy's propensity to get sick happened to strike here while he was at Camp Kilmer, his entire future might well have been radically different. He arrived at Kilmer in the company of only three of his four buddies whom he had met at Camp Wolters. One of them had stayed behind at Fort Meade to have emergency surgery and so was laid up when his companions, including Murphy, were transferred to New Jersey in preparation for deployment. While Murphy and the rest went to North Africa, once he had recovered the Army sent him not to Europe but to Newfoundland where he spent the entire war. It's hard to imagine what might have awaited Audie Murphy in a post such as that, but it would have been difficult to become the most decorated soldier in U.S. history that far from the front. His life would have been completely different.

He stayed well, however, and when his orders came through he was more than ready to move. At Kilmer the men were divided into platoons of sixty-five soldiers each. Murphy's platoon commander was Second Lieutenant W. Heard Reeves from Wichita Falls, Texas, who had been drafted in January 1941. In less than two years, Reeves would be pinning Murphy's Second Lieutenant insignia on his uniform in France. Now, however, he gave Murphy his first military promotion, albeit a temporary one, as a corporal to assist Reeves aboard ship until they reached their destination.

On Monday morning, February 8, 1943, Audie Murphy boarded the U.S. Army transport ship *Hawaiian Shipper,* a single-funnel grey converted freighter making its first transit as a troop ship. That evening the ship headed into the Atlantic to rendezvous with its convoy of other troop ships and an escort screen of destroyers. Now that they were at sea, the troops were given their orders: they were heading for North Africa to join the fight against the Germans.

# CHAPTER THREE

# INTO THE FIGHT

D uring most of the eleven days it took the convoy to cross the Atlantic Ocean, Audie Murphy was terribly seasick. He was far from alone. For most of these new soldiers it was their first time at sea. Though the ship conducted numerous submarine drills, the lookouts spotted no German subs, and the convoy made the transit without incident. The troops landed at the port of Casablanca on February 20, 1943, and then were loaded aboard a train for a sixty-mile trip north to the city of Rabat, headquarters for all replacement assignment and deployment in North Africa. Murphy was classified as a Browning Automatic Rifle (BAR) specialist and assigned to Company B, 1st Battalion, 15th Infantry Regiment, of the 3rd Infantry Division. This unit would be his home for the remainder of the war.

The 3rd was one of the legendary divisions in the U.S. Army. Since 1918, it had been known as "The Rock of the Marne" in honor of its stalwart action against the German offensive at the Marne River in WWI. In November 1942 the division stormed into Morocco as part of the TORCH landings. "You must succeed," General George S. Patton told the division before it entered into combat against the Vichy French, "for to retreat is as cowardly as it is fatal." In little more than a week, the Allies succeeded in occupying Morocco but at a cost of over 1,100 U.S. casualties. The fighting had moved onto Tunisia, where Americans were now fighting the German Afrika Korps commanded by Field Marshal Erwin Rommel, "the Desert Fox."

Troops newly assigned to the 3rd Division marched to its headquarters at Port Lyautey on the northwestern coast of Morocco. Murphy thought it was "nice here in Africa" and said "I never felt better in my life." His duties did not extend much beyond drilling. A fellow Texan in his regiment noted that "There wasn't much to do except guard duty."[1]

Like so many other soldiers, Audie Murphy filled some of his spare time by playing cards and throwing dice, proving himself a natural gambler. "The first time I saw Audie he was raking in a pile of money," said one of his fellow soldiers. Gambling remained one of the passions of his life, one that eventually became a problem.[2]

Taking command of the 3rd Division in March 1943 was Major General Lucian K. Truscott. Truscott, a Texan from Navarro County, just south of Dallas, was one of the finest combat commanders the army had. A stern disciplinarian, he was known for the intensity with which he trained his men. The quick pace of his grueling training marches became known as the "Truscott Trot." "I cursed every step," said Private Milton Robertson, who had been with Murphy since Camp Wolters. The "trot" had its purpose. Truscott wanted infantry that could move fast.[3]

Truscott thought American troops were "hunters by instinct," and wanted his subordinate officers to instill that feeling into their men before every battle. For Private Audie Murphy that was certainly true and he was eager to see how his Hunt County sharpshooting would translate to the battlefield.

The division trained in Algeria for an as yet unspecified assault. But there was clearly something coming. "I hope to see a little action soon," Murphy wrote his sister Corinne.[4] Rumor had it that his regiment would take part in the final push against the Afrika Korps in Tunisia. The rumors proved false. Instead of seeing combat in North Africa, Murphy was charged with guarding German prisoners, after the Afrika Korps surrendered on May 9.

Tens of thousands of German and Italian prisoners flowed into hastily constructed camps, ultimately more than 250,000 of them. Many were eventually sent to prisoner of war camps in the United States, which, as General Omar Bradley told General Dwight Eisenhower, was unpopular with the troops: "Our troops get mad when they hear we're shipping PW's back to the states." The troops did not think they were fighting so that German and Italian prisoners could sit out the war in America.

————————

More than 18,500 American soldiers were killed or wounded in the North African campaign, and the American army learned some harsh lessons. One was how badly many new troops had been trained. By some accounts, as many as 80 percent were not qualified for the weapons they were assigned. Still others were in less than ideal physical condition; almost half of one group of 250 replacements hustled to the front were thirty-nine years old or older. Some commanders were also troubled about the prevalence of "battle fatigue," what in the First World War had been called "shell shock." One combat hospital in North Africa reported handling more than 1,700 cases.

Murphy saw cases of battle fatigue, but dismissed them, as many did, as a simple failure of nerve, mere cowardice.

More than 500,000 American troops were now in North Africa, and if Murphy's regiment had not seen combat, simple proximity to the action had intensified his preparation. Murphy said, "I learned more in three months of training in Africa than I learned in six months in the States." General Truscott boasted that "Never was any division more fit for combat" than the 3rd Division in North Africa. It was one of five U.S. Army divisions organized into the Seventh Army under the command of General George S. Patton and readied for the invasion of Sicily.[5]

The invasion force for what was labeled Operation HUSKY was enormous—3,000 ships, with two armies, one American and one British, of 80,000 men each. "There is no way of conveying the enormous size of that fleet," wrote the famous American war correspondent Ernie Pyle. "On the horizon it resembled a distant city." Admiral Kent Hewitt who was in command called it "the most gigantic fleet in the world's history." Most of the soldiers involved had no real idea of where they were headed when they boarded the ships, although rumors abounded. Only after they were at sea did they learn they were heading for Sicily, where Allied planners estimated that 300,000 German and Italian troops were waiting.[6]

The plan was for the British troops to hit the southeastern corner of the island around the ancient city of Syracuse, then pivot north and move up the eastern coastline toward the city of Messina at the narrowest point of the straits separating the island from mainland Italy. Meanwhile the Americans would hit the island's southern shore and then move inland, covering the left flank of the British army. "The first day at sea was like a peacetime Mediterranean cruise," Pyle said. A storm, however, turned the crossing into chaos, knocking ships off course, but also grounding German air reconnaissance.[7]

As the ship on which he was sailing approached the coast of Sicily in the tossing waves, Audie Murphy was among the many who had yet to see any combat, yet to have a shot fired at him in anger. Prepared as he may have been, the experience of fighting was still a great unknown; mentally he was unprepared for what awaited him. Green troops, said John Steinbeck (who, like Murphy, traveled on a troop ship in the Mediterranean, in his case covering the war for the *New York Herald Tribune*), lacked only one thing to make them soldiers: enemy fire, "and they will never be soldiers until they have it. No one, least of all themselves, knows what they will do when the terrible thing happens. No man there knows whether he can take it, knows whether he will run away or stick, or lose his nerve and go to pieces, or will be a good soldier." At this point, how Murphy himself would react was anyone's guess.[8]

As suddenly as it came, the storm departed, leaving the armada to close in on the south coast of Sicily. H-Hour for the 3rd Division in Sicily was 0245 on July 10, 1943. With battle looming, the rumble of the ship's engines died away. Big search lights from on shore swept the still water but the feared shore batteries never opened up, even as the assault craft made their perilous way to the beach.

Audie Murphy's division was to secure the western edge of the American beachhead around Licata, a coastal town of about 35,000. The beaches here were neither mined nor booby-trapped, and German air assaults were sporadic. Ten battalions went ashore in the first hour along with scores of tanks. Fifteen miles to the east, around the town of Gela, the 1st Infantry Division had a rougher reception coming ashore, as did the 45th Division farther east.

Murphy's Company B hit the beach around 0800. This was Audie Murphy's first time in combat and even the relatively small number of casualties on the beach shocked him. "I thought that some outfit had been massacred."[9] Under fire himself, he was cool. "From various

points came the rattle of small arms, but we soon got used to that."
His battalion was to pass through the units that had already secured
the beachhead, and move quickly to the "yellow line," an imaginary
boundary that snaked along the rough terrain anywhere from 10 to
30 miles inland. Taking the line was crucial because from that point
enemy artillery fire could no longer reach the beaches.

As daylight broke over the town of Licata, Admiral Hewitt spotted an American flag rising above a small fort that was a key target
of the Army Rangers. By now, American troops and Hewitt's naval
batteries had knocked out the enemy's artillery. At sunset on D-Day,
things in Murphy's sector were days ahead of schedule. The first night
ashore he and his company rested on a hillside north of town. Within
two days there were upwards of 80,000 Allied troops ashore. By then,
Murphy and Company B had already passed their portion of the
"yellow line" and were almost fifteen miles inland.

The Sicilian terrain was notable mostly for its dust. The white
chalky dust was so fine, so ubiquitous, and formed clouds so thick
that when troops marched through it they were often obscured from
the waist down. The dust clung to their exposed skin, making them
look "like clowns at a circus."[10]

Murphy and his company had fallen out for a rest when, among
the constant din of artillery fire to which they were already becoming
accustomed, there was a suddenly different-sounding incoming shell.
"Something terrible and immediate about its whistle makes my scalp
start prickling," Murphy wrote, recounting the experience. "I grab
my helmet and flip over on my stomach. The explosion is thunderous.
Steel fragments whine, and the ground seems to jump up and hit me
in the face." Before the explosion a soldier with his helmet off had
been sitting on a rock nearby; after the explosion, he was dead, a
trickle of blood from his mouth and nose the only outward sign of
violence. "So it happens as easily as that," Murphy reflected. "How

do you put skill against skill if you cannot even see the enemy?" he wondered. "Where is the expected adventure?" asked the young boy who first dreamed of combat as a way out of the cotton fields. At least he had not broken. At least he was not a coward.[11]

Audie Murphy also killed his first enemy soldiers in Sicily. He was out in front of his company with a few other scouts, watching for mines, traps, and snipers. Two Italian officers suddenly sprang up from cover and leaped on horses to escape. His reaction, he said, was simply the instinctive one of a hunter who is stalking a rabbit that suddenly bolts. He dropped to a knee, took a bead, and brought them down with one shot each. "That's our job, isn't it," he responded when a lieutenant asked him why he shot them when they were clearly running away. "They would have killed us if they'd had the chance." Murphy thought that while it was difficult for a person to shed the conviction that human life is sacred, he himself did so at that precise moment. "Now I have shed my first blood," he said. "I feel no qualms; no pride; no remorse. There is only a weary indifference that will follow me through the war." It would follow him the rest of his life.[12]

On Sicily he more than once looked into the face of a cowardly soldier "and found it loathsome." When toward the end of the campaign his company was pinned down along a river, one of the men began crying hysterically. He was dispatched to the rear. Murphy and the others watched him go "with hatred in our eyes." "I have seen war as it actually is," Murphy wrote, "and I do not like it." But he also had no respect for those could not take it.[13]

Company B met its first real resistance near the village of Campobello, and Murphy came under direct and sustained enemy fire. On July 13, 1943, his platoon was pinned down by machine gun fire on a dusty hillside. Suddenly he jumped up and "started firing from the hip," charging at the enemy, and yelling for the rest of the men in the platoon to follow him. "He was that kind of soldier," said his platoon commander. Two days later he was promoted to corporal, and given front line duty, which is exactly what he wanted. "You may have to take over a squad," his captain warned him.[14]

Bill Mauldin, who drew one of the most famous comic strips of the war, "Willie and Joe," said that in war "nobody really knows what he's doing." If he had seen Audie Murphy in action, he might have thought differently. Murphy had an instinct for combat. "If I discovered one valuable thing during my early combat days," Murphy said, "it was audacity, which is often mistaken for courage or foolishness. It is neither. Audacity is a tactical weapon. Nine times out of ten it will throw the enemy off balance and confuse him. However much one sees of audacious deeds, nobody really expects them. They are not in the rule books. I found that retreating was the most dangerous maneuver possible.... If you have no defense, attack."[15]

As American soldiers pressed northward, many native Sicilians responded warmly to them. Their attitude "was more that of a liberated people than was the case in French North Africa," wrote Ernie Pyle, who had come ashore and was now travelling with the 3rd Division. Hastily painted banners proclaiming "Welcome" in English were tacked to buildings. Grateful villagers showered American troops with figs, peaches, grapes, wine, and hazelnuts. Grapevines were heavy with fruit and there were more watermelons than Pyle had ever seen in his life. Every camp had at least one hundred-pound bag of almonds from which the troops munched continually. There were endless fields of ripe tomatoes, many of which eventually made their way to the tables of captains and generals who were now busily planning the next step of the campaign.[16]

As had happened more than once in training, Murphy's youthful appearance—his "cursed baby face," he called it—nearly got him taken out of the action again. Hardly had the invasion of Sicily gotten underway before his company commander transferred him to HQ to be a runner. He rebelled against it, and every chance he got, he joined patrols and otherwise sought action. Finally his captain relented. He would be on the front lines for the next step of the campaign.

———————

The roads in Sicily turned out to be appallingly bad, and the invading Allied armies found their progress impeded not just by the enemy but by clogged roads. To restore mobility on the American front, General George S. Patton made a dash northwest to seize the ancient Sicilian capital of Palermo. Don't stop for anything but gas, Patton told General Truscott. He wanted the 3rd Division to be in Palermo in five days.[17]

The hundred-mile drive to Palermo "became virtually a foot race," Murphy noted, as his regiment hustled through one dusty town after another. There were minefields to negotiate and resistance that varied from desultory artillery shelling to seemingly limitless small arms fire. The terrain was rugged, the roads rocky, but the Truscott Trot kept the men moving along at a clip of twenty-five to thirty miles each day, while accepting the surrender of hundreds of Italian troops.[18]

Audie found at one point that he could not keep up. He felt feverish and collapsed by the roadside, vomiting. Yet he eventually picked himself up and rejoined his company. The next day, he suddenly blacked out. He woke up in an aide station shivering and sweating. In *To Hell and Back*, his memoir of his combat years, Murphy implies that he was down with malaria, a common enough ailment among the Allied troops in Sicily, but he was actually diagnosed with a respiratory illness, and he spent more than a week in the hospital before he could rejoin his company.

After the fall of Palermo, the 3rd Infantry Division was assigned to support the 45th Infantry Division on the final drive from Palermo to Messina, across whose strait is the Italian mainland. The retreating Germans were seasoned troops who lived up to their formidable reputation, making this the costliest segment of the campaign.

Murphy and his regiment finally reached the Furiano River. The riverbed itself had been mined and the Germans were in position to keep the Americans under near constant fire, including mortar and artillery fire. Once again, Murphy saw an American soldier lose his nerve, break into noisy sobs, and be sent to the rear. One of Murphy's buddies said, "If I ever throw a whingding like that, shoot me." "Gladly," Murphy replied.[19]

Murphy had no fear of combat, but he also no longer worried about being held back occasionally on guard duty. "I see now that the fighting will not run out," he said. "There will be plenty of war for everybody."

Finally on the morning of August 17, 1943, the last German soldier left Messina and the American flag flew over the city. The entire island was now in the hands of the Allies.

Had the war ended here, or had a random artillery shell exploded in a slightly different place and either killed him or sent him home with a "million-dollar wound," the story of Audie Murphy would have been unremarkable. But his moment had not yet arrived. Heroism, particularly of the kind that shaped Audie Murphy's life, often comes in a flash. Others had had their moment by the end of the Sicily campaign; men from the ranks of the 3rd Division—which would become the most decorated division in the entire war—were already being awarded the Congressional Medal of Honor. There was no shortage of bravery on Sicily. Audie Murphy had proven himself a sound soldier, but as the war moved to Italy, he remained just another G.I.

# CHAPTER FOUR

# ITALY

E arly in the morning of September 9, 1943, the American invasion of Italy, Operation AVALANCHE, came ashore near the city of Salerno, on a great curving bay roughly midway between the toe of Italy and Rome. Once again, the ships of the invading armada were under the command of Admiral Hewitt, who, along with Fifth Army Commander General Mark Clark, could now do nothing but wait and hope as thousands of men climbed down into the hundreds of plywood landing craft called "Higgins boats" that were riding easily on the low swells of the dark sea. Their engines rumbling across the quiet pre-dawn water, countless boats headed in toward the shore, where German troops waited with nervous fingers on triggers.

As had been the case at Sicily, Audie Murphy was not in the first wave hitting the beach. In AVALANCHE, the U.S. 3rd Division was designated as the reserve for commanders to put into the action when and where it was most needed. It was needed soon because the fighting was rough. Unknown to the Americans, there were 135,000 Germans in the south of Italy and they began moving heavy reinforcements to the area around Salerno less than twenty-four hours after the American invasion began. A worried Eisenhower acknowledged that the battle for Salerno would "be a matter of touch and go for the next few days."[1]

Eventually the Americans managed to hold on to the beach, but it required ten days of hard fighting to take Salerno. When Audie Murphy and his company landed in Italy on September 21, just south of Salerno at Battipaglia, he described the apparently secure beachhead as having been "bought dearly with the blood and guts of the men who preceded us." Indeed, more than 1,200 American soldiers were killed in action and thousands more had been wounded in the ten-day campaign.[2]

Once his unit got ashore, "we were prepared for a quick dash to Rome," Murphy said, but the reality was completely different. Instead, he found himself pinned down in a muddy ditch by German machine gun fire. At his side was Lattie Tipton, a private from Tennessee, and a soldier almost as full of dash and daring as Murphy himself. They kept their heads down and drew up a quick plan. With grenades and rifles, and a full measure of audacity, he and Tipton cleared out the enemy position.

Finally, on October 1, 1943, the Allies rolled into the city of Naples to the joy of the elated residents who threw flowers—and often themselves—at the Americans' feet. The Germans had done their best to destroy the port facilities as they retreated and the harbor was choked with sunken ships, many of which had been scuttled. For days afterward, time bombs that the Germans had left behind devastated the town and killed Allied soldiers and civilians alike.

Meanwhile, twenty miles to the north, Audie Murphy and the men of Company B were closing in on the first natural barrier to their progress. The wide and shallow Volturno River was the first major river crossing that the Allies would have to make in Europe. On the far side, 35,000 Germans lay in wait. Here General Truscott sent his 3rd Division into action.

Unlike the dusty, hot Sicilian campaign, the Italian campaign was fought in mud—the seasonal autumn rains had begun shortly before the fall of Naples. "Rain, rain, rain," General John Lucas, commander of VI Corps (under which the 3rd Division operated) wrote in his diary. "Enemy resistance is not nearly as great as that of Mother Nature." The mud was everywhere. But there were compensations. The soldiers discovered that apples in Italy were what the tomatoes and watermelon had been in Sicily—everywhere in abundance. This was not a land of bucolic orchards and gently rolling fields, however. Picturesque as it may have been, the terrain heavily favored the defender, even more than on the north coast of Sicily.[3]

The Volturno River, generally shallow, was now swollen and flowing swiftly because of the continual autumn rains. Early one evening as Murphy and a few of his buddies crept toward the river, they discovered a small muddy cave that some German troops had dug out when they had been stationed on the south bank. "The sour stench of decaying food and moldy clothing tells us that the Germans have been up to their usual job of bad housekeeping," he remarked caustically. It was also ridden with fleas, which kept them scratching for days. Nevertheless it was a good position, with no traps inside and a sandbag wall to shield the opening from enemy fire. More importantly, it was big enough for several men to shelter in while they took turns keeping watch, peering across the river through the constant rain for any sign of enemy troops, and passing the time shooting craps for small stakes.[4]

General Lucas was hesitant to send the 3rd Division across the river by itself, so Murphy and the rest of the soldiers had to wait while the 45th came up and got into position, which, it was assumed, could take awhile. "There is no way of knowing how long we will be here," Murphy said.

The time, however, was not wasted. While combat bonds men, so does waiting for it—and Murphy bonded closer to his small circle of friends during their watches through the cold, drizzly nights. He told them about his siblings in the orphanage and his determination to get them out after the war. He also talked about his mother—"he'd almost come to tears talking about his mother," a buddy remembered. His closest friend was Lattie Tipton. "We were like brothers," Murphy said. It was actually the sort of friendship he sought to avoid, he later admitted, "because most likely it was going to end tomorrow." Tipton, he said, "was the one man who kept me from being afraid."[5]

Another close friend was Joe Sieja, a Polish émigré who had joined the Army after only five years in America. He had an intense hatred of the Germans, and in his eyes, Murphy said, was "a strange, broken light which heightens the habitual sadness of his features." Having only a small circle of friends with whom he was intimate would be a characteristic that Audie Murphy would carry with him throughout his time in the Army, and then after into civilian life.[6]

Murphy rarely received letters, and when buddies asked him if he had girl back home, his stock response was "I never had the chance to fall in love." He was "too damned proud," he said, "to let a girl see the patches on my pants." But Tipton often shared his letters from home, including letters from his ex-wife. "We got married too young," He confided to his friend one night, "and the big things I planned didn't pan out." Tipton had a nine-year-old daughter about whom he talked lovingly, and whose image popped into Murphy's mind every time his friend took a risk. "I see the eyes, eager with life; her pert freckled nose; her pigtails with bows at the ends." Murphy grew grimly determined that his friend would see his daughter and ex-wife again.[7]

One historian has commented that Audie Murphy had "an almost fanatical sense of responsibility." He was "fiercely loyal to those who'd befriended him or for whom he was responsible." Buddies remember that he would often carry the pack or the gun of a man who was too exhausted to go on. Tipton, however, stubbornly ignored all his friend's attempts to keep him from taking any wild risks.[8]

Murphy and his buddies could often hear the Germans talking across the river when the air was still. Sometimes the sentries yelled taunts back and forth in the darkness. Since his days in basic training, one of his buddies remembered, Audie Murphy had shown an uncanny ability to spot bad camouflage. It was an ability that had helped him as a hunter back home tracking rabbits and squirrels; now it served him well along the river. Far across the river he spotted what he called "a curious shrub in a thicket. Its leaves seem to be turned the wrong way." He picked up a rifle and shot at it. Retaliatory bullets popped into their sandbags.

The waiting continued. Murphy and his buddies had been dug in without resupply for three days. They had food enough, plenty of rations, but their water was running out and they were afraid to eat lest it aggravate their thirst. Enemy snipers made it too dangerous to get water from the river. In the flickering light of a candle, the men's eyes shone "like the eyes of caged animals." Tempers grew short and they began to quarrel with one another. Finally, the sound of the gurgling water grew hard to resist, and one of Murphy's buddies broke for the river to fill his canteen. The others yelled frantically for him to come back. A burst from a German machine gun crumpled him halfway down the slope. There his broken body stayed as the rain continued to fall.

---

At last, word came down from HQ that the river crossing was set for the night of October 13. The 3rd Division was to make a feint, drawing German units away from main crossing sites downstream. At midnight, American artillery opened up with a two hour barrage, followed by smoke shells to cover the infantry as they crossed the river under a bright full moon, their helmets gleaming white with frost. Murphy's company remained in a support position, crossing the river the next morning. By the time the river crossing was made and the position secured, the 3rd Division had lost 300 men. The Germans fell back to the Apennine Mountains and their next defensive position, the "Gustav Line," anchored in part by the rock promontory on which sat the medieval monastery of Monte Cassino.

As the Americans pushed forward, the rains increased and it turned sharply colder. The terrain became more formidable. The ever-present mud made the steep rocky ridges treacherous to navigate, even for the mules that now picked their way back down the mountains with dead soldiers lashed to their backs. It was "a nightmare for offensive troops," Murphy said. Ernie Pyle, who was now travelling with the 3rd Division, observed that "a mere platoon of Germans, well dug in on a high, rock-spined hill, could hold out for a long time against tremendous onslaughts." Artillery shells bursting among the rocks turned the rocks themselves into deadly shrapnel. In one battalion, 15 percent of the casualties were from shards of flying rock. The infantry "lived like men of prehistoric times, and a club would have become them more than a machine gun." Wars "should be fought in better country than this," General Lucas remarked wearily.[9]

The constant fighting, the continual scrambling through the mud and over the hills, took a relentless toll on the men. "War is without beginning, without end," Murphy said of the campaign. "It goes on forever." Ernie Pyle noted that "Outside of the occasional peaks of bitter fighting and heavy casualties that highlight military operations, I believe the outstanding trait in any campaign is the terrible weariness that gradually comes over everybody." It was, he said, a "stage of exhaustion that is incomprehensible to folks back home."[10]

"Crawling with filth and sodden with weariness," Murphy's regiment came out of the lines on November 17, 1943. They had been at the front for sixty days. Trudging from the front lines to the rear area they passed by a company of replacements heading to the front. "All are subdued," the veterans noted, and "a few are plainly white-faced, dry-mouthed with fear." Here were men facing the same basic question about fear and courage that every soldier in every age had to face. Audie Murphy faced it in a boat approaching Sicily, and now he had been permanently changed by the answer. "We regard them with casual interest," he said. "Pity is a luxury we cannot afford."[11]

The men of Company B went into camp east of Naples where they rested, helped train replacements, and underwent more amphibious assault practice. In December 1943, Murphy was promoted to sergeant, a promotion he regarded more as a tribute to his mere survival than anything else, in an Italian campaign that ended with more than 310,000 Allied casualties. Avoiding death felt like little more than dumb luck. Murphy wrote that by now he and his buddies felt like old men, "fugitives from the law of averages," as he put it. Bound together by their experience in combat, Murphy and his companions grew to be bitterly suspicious and resentful of replacements, of the men who had not shared their sacrifice. If they lasted long enough to prove themselves, they would slowly become accepted. If they challenged Murphy's orders, as one replacement later did, the response was swift, a punch to the stomach and the jaw, and a smashing of the man's head into the ground until bystanders pulled Murphy off. Patience, too, was a casualty of war.[12]

───────────

"The stagnation of the whole campaign on the Italian front is scandalous," Winston Churchill said in December 1943. The stalemate south of Monte Cassino was the last straw, and Murphy and the 3rd Division became part of the operation to break it. The plan was to land Allied troops somewhere north of the Gustav Line, forcing the Germans to abandon the position and fall back. As they studied the maps, the eyes of planners were drawn to a small curving bay less than forty miles south of Rome on which lay the resort city of Anzio. Conditions there looked perfect for an assault across the beach and maybe a subsequent thrust to Rome before the Germans could reinforce the city. "I have many misgivings," VI Corps commander General Lucas remarked about the Anzio operation, worried that the general assessment of what the Germans would do in response to the landings was too specific and too optimistic. "Apparently everyone was in on the secret of the German intentions except me," he said.[13]

Truscott's 3rd Division was selected to lead the attack, now codenamed SHINGLE. The men spent three days practicing beach landings, while General Mark Clark worried over what he thought was an appalling loss of the division's equipment in training exercises and blamed it on "overwhelming mismanagement by the navy." General Lucas was not happy either. "The army has gone nuts again," he confided to his diary. "The general idea seems to be that the Germans are licked and are fleeing in disorder and nothing remains but to mop up." He worried that "they will end up by putting me ashore with inadequate force and get me in a serious jam."

As chaplains held services and veterans recognized something big was about to happen, Audie Murphy came down with malaria. He tried to push through it, shivering and sweating. "If I go to the infirmary," he worried, "I think it will seem I am deliberately trying to avoid the coming action." Finally his illness became too obvious to ignore. A buddy reported his condition to his commander and his CO ordered him to report to the infirmary where doctors discovered he was running a fever of 105. They set him down on a cot and once again he blacked out.[14]

Murphy awoke in a hospital in Naples. To his frustration, the nurses could tell him nothing of what had happened to the 3rd Division at Anzio and would only pump him full of foul-tasting medicine. He wanted desperately to rejoin his unit, even though he would later admit that it was always harder to go back to the front lines after a hospital stay. "Lying there in the hospital, a man has too much time think," one of his buddies once said to him. "And that's bad. He gets in the mood to live again." Murphy understood the remark, but was always determined to get back to his buddies.[15]

Once he recovered, Audie Murphy arrived at Anzio a week later with a detachment of replacements and made his way to B Company headquarters, which by then was set up just inland from the beach in a battered farmhouse. He discovered that his company had taken a pounding in the landing and had suffered many casualties. Among them was Joe Sieja, Murphy's Polish buddy, who had been killed on the third day by a German 88mm artillery shell. Murphy, the survivor, was now promoted to Staff Sergeant.[16]

Contrary to Allied hopes, there was no swift breakout from the beaches at Anzio. It soon became yet another frustrating and bloody stalemate. The frontline trenches, the foxholes, the rear areas, the entire beachhead were all under constant bombardment from German artillery. Incoming fire hit hospitals, supply dumps, and mess halls equally. "Bakers and typewriter repairmen and clerks were not immune from shells and bombs," said Ernie Pyle.[17]

Murphy's commanding officers had come to depend on his uncanny ability to move quietly to carry out reconnaissance patrols between the American and the German lines, and that skill was crucial at Anzio. Creeping out between the lines made him think of home. "As a farm youngster," he said, "the land meant either hunger or bread to me. Now its shape is the difference between life and death. Every roll, depression, rock, or tree is significant." In one such patrol, Murphy's ears told him the Germans were "going in deep for a defensive stand. The throttled-down churn of engines and a cautious clanking of steel tell us that tanks are being sneaked into the area."[18]

Throughout the Anzio operation Murphy also repeatedly volunteered for what were called "conversation and capture" patrols, which involved seizing a German soldier and bringing him back for interrogation. Murphy could literally sniff out Germans by the distinctive smell of their tobacco.

Finally a breakout attack was planned against Cisterna, an important German communications center. It kicked off at 0200 on January 30, 1944. "Like robots driven by coiled springs, we again move forward," Murphy wrote. The 1st and 3rd Ranger Battalions led the attack and by dawn had closed to within a few hundred yards of the town. But even as the Germans gave way before them, the Rangers were moving into a trap, a cul-de-sac, in which they became surrounded by enemy fire. With the Rangers pinned down, Murphy's Company B was rushed in to rescue them, but had to cross minefields and interlocking fields of German fire. It was brutal. "The fiery blanket woven by their guns never lifts," Murphy wrote. "We may as well be hurtling naked bodies against a wall of spears."[19]

His Company was finally ordered to withdraw. "Not a yard of ground was gained by the murderous three days of assault," he noted bitterly. The official 3rd Division historian called Cisterna "the most savage and disappointing action the Division had fought up until that time." For the next two months, the men of the 3rd Division fought a defensive war of trenches. Men lived in dugout caves beneath parked Sherman tanks because when they dug regular fox-holes they immediately filled with water. Others had to bail out their flooded foxholes with their helmets. Trench foot was rampant. "It was the only time during the war that I felt we were all doomed," Murphy said.

After the First Battle of Cisterna, Murphy was given command of Company B's third platoon. The incessant fighting, the unpredict-able and terrifying artillery barrages meant that fear was a constant companion even for a seasoned soldier like Murphy. "It strikes first in the stomach, coming like the disemboweling hand that is thrust into the carcass of a chicken. I feel now as though icy fingers have reached into my mid-parts and twisted the intestines into knots." His growing familiarity with fear was even changing the way he dealt with other soldiers who were feeling it. "Now there'll be times when you'll be scared to death," he later told a replacement. "I'm always scared when we're up front. Don't be ashamed of it. There'll be times that you want to cry. There's nothing wrong with that."[20]

The ground around Anzio was flat and muddy; much of it was reclaimed swampland that flooded with the slightest rains, which had the one advantage of limiting the mobility of heavy German tanks. But eventually the rains stopped and the roads began to dry out. One morn-ing in early March, as he was scanning the surrounding landscape with binoculars, Murphy spotted a Mark VI Tiger tank moving up the road. More appeared behind that one—twenty in all. He called in artillery, staying on the line and correcting the incoming fire until the first tank was hit. The others, now blocked from proceeding, withdrew. Murphy understood, however, that this was only a temporary respite.

Under cover of night, he led a squad to destroy the incapacitated tank before the Germans could repair it. About a hundred yards from the road, Murphy ordered his men to cover him, while he crawled forward alone. He hurled a grenade through the tank's open hatch and followed that up with rifle grenades, permanently disabling it. German sentries responded with machine gun fire, and Murphy retreated with tracer bullets slashing through the darkness just above his head. For this action, Murphy won his first decoration for valor: the Bronze Star with "V" device.

On April 21, 1944, Audie Murphy's name first appeared in the Greenville, Texas, newspapers. "Greenville Boy Enjoys Reprieve From Stay in Wet Slit Trench," announced the headline. The story did not mention Murphy's Bronze Star (though it did mention his promotion to staff sergeant), but instead focused on the dismal, muddy conditions at Anzio and the relief that came from just a moment's respite from the front.[21]

One evening less than two weeks later, as Murphy headed out on his regular rounds to check on the company's machine gun posts, he suddenly reeled and blacked out. Before he regained consciousness two buddies carried him back to an aid station where he was diagnosed with a severe case of influenza. As he recovered, he had a flirtatious relationship with a blonde-haired, blue-eyed nurse who in his book *To Hell and Back* he called Helen. She was one of the few people, besides his closest friends, with whom he felt he could relax and talk. He told her that he had had a "bellyful" of combat, but he had no inclination to quit now. His buddies were too important to him. "They bitch; they cuss; they foul up. But when the chips are down, they do their jobs like men," he said. "As long as there's a man in the lines, maybe I feel that my place is up there beside him."[22]

On May 21, 1944, he was back in the front lines when Company B was ordered into the fray for the hard fighting of what would come to be called the Second Battle of Cisterna, as once again American troops tried to break through the German lines. The 15th Regiment achieved its first and second phase objectives, but then disaster struck. On May 26 his unit was bombed and strafed by American aircraft that mistook them for German troops. The friendly fire inflicted more than 100 casualties on the 15th Regiment but none in Murphy's Company B.

The offensive continued forward. As his men moved out to cut a crucial railroad line south of Cisterna, Murphy remarked "we must keep hitting the Germans while they are still off-balance." Finally American firepower overwhelmed the Germans. Their lines crumbled and the tide abruptly turned. Months of stalemate washed away. After the breakout at the Second Battle of Cisterna, Audie Murphy received two more decorations for combat: a combat infantryman badge (for which he had become eligible in Sicily the previous summer) and his first Oak Leaf Cluster.

"Oh, gather 'round me comrades; and listen while I speak," Murphy wrote in his memoir, although attributing the poetry to someone else:

> Along the shore the cannons roar.
> Oh how can a soldier sleep?
> The going's slow on Anzio.
> And hell is six feet deep.
> Praise be to God for this captured sod
> That rich with blood does seep;
> With yours and mine, like butchered swine's;
> And hell is six feet deep.

Rome at last fell to the Americans on June 4, 1944, and on June 6, as Americans were storming across the beaches in Northern

France, the 3rd Division was assigned to garrison duty in the Eternal City. The Italians greeted the American arrival as a liberation. "Everyone was out on the streets," wrote American journalist Eric Sevareid, "thousands upon thousands from the outlying areas walking toward the center of the city." It was a "monstrous crowd." Sevareid was riding in an American jeep "while flowers rained upon our heads, men grabbed and kissed our hands, old women burst into tears, and girls and boys wanted to climb up beside us." A sergeant commented that "young girls kissed every soldier they could lay their hands on and one tiny blond succeeded in mounting the turret gun of a light tank."[23]

The 3rd Division set up its command post at the Sapienza University of Rome, much of which had been severely damaged by bombing the previous summer. Murphy and the men of Company B pitched their tents in a nearby public park. Like many of his buddies, Audie was not impressed with Rome. Its public services had been destroyed. There were shortages of food, medicine, and fresh water. "Getting washed regularly was a luxury for all but the privileged living in the neighborhoods taken over by the German commands," one witness reported. Lice were everywhere, as unavoidable as the sickening odor of the chemical used to treat them.[24]

Murphy was also contending with the numbing effect of the combat he had experienced. "We prowl through Rome like ghosts," he said, taking note that he felt no satisfaction in anything he saw or did. "I feel like a man briefly reprieved from death; and there is no joy within me." His thoughts were less on his temporary reprieve from combat and more on those who were still enduring it. "We can have no hope until the war is ended. Thinking of the men on the fighting fronts, I grow lonely on the streets of Rome."[25]

Less than two weeks later the whole division was pulled out of Rome and sent to Naples to begin intensive training for still another amphibious operation; even though the veterans in the division had been through several by now, most of the new men had not. While in Naples, Audie Murphy turned nineteen—he had been in the front lines of combat for a year now. Here Murphy honed his skill as an artillery spotter, working with the 39th Field Artillery near the coastal town of Pozzuoli. His observation post was on a sand dune. Peering through binoculars, he estimated the distance of a large raft anchored at sea, which estimate a radio operator then relayed to the artillery. His second, corrected estimate was a bull's-eye. Colonel Henry Bodson, in charge of the training, could hardly believe how Murphy's "estimate of range change was perfect." It was a skill that would soon contribute to his fame.[26]

# A ROAD TO HEROISM

t the beginning of World War II, most Army doctors believed that what was then called "combat fatigue" was a condition that simply did not occur in normal soldiers. The prevailing wisdom was that it resulted from an underlying and pre-existing emotional instability. A sharp program of careful screening could weed out the weaker men who were susceptible both to it and to various other psychiatric illnesses, and therefore prevent its occurrence on the battlefield. It was not until Army doctors started analyzing the data gathered from the shocking number of battle fatigue cases that occurred in the relatively short North African campaign that they began to acknowledge that their assumptions were not panning out the way they expected.[1]

That it was the men who were veterans of the toughest combat who were showing symptoms of battle fatigue far more frequently than were fresh and inexperienced troops, made it clear that the condition was not one of simply going to pieces at the first exposure to the violence of war. Also, the grim fact of combat could be assumed to have weeded out all the "weaklings," wrote one Army doctor. "The men who remained had proved the toughness of their underlying personality structure by their mere survival." Instead of psychoneurosis (as they called it) being a predictable malady, doctors started acknowledging that anyone could develop it under certain conditions.

The most important of these conditions was the length of battle trauma, "that is, number of consecutive days in action." This was followed by physical fatigue, due not only to improper sleep, prolonged exertion, and irregular eating, but fatigue that was exacerbated by recurrent bouts of illness such as malaria and influenza. Other triggers of battle trauma included "explosions in close vicinity," and the "observation of death and maiming of buddies." It was a description that, by the summer of 1944, told the story of Sergeant Audie L. Murphy of the 3rd Infantry Division with startling accuracy. While Murphy showed few symptoms during the war, from June to November 1944 one in four soldiers fighting in France was treated for some kind of battle fatigue. In all, Army doctors diagnosed nearly a million cases of it.[2]

---

Audie Murphy went back into combat again as part of the second invasion of France. Operation DRAGOON was aimed at the coast of southern France with the objectives of both seizing the ports at Marseilles and Toulon and stretching German defenses to the breaking point. The 3rd Division was designated as one of the three American divisions, along with the 45th and the 36th (a unit of the Texas National Guard Audie Murphy would join after the war) that would make the assault under VI Corps commander General Lucian Truscott.

As had been the case with the famous Normandy landing a month earlier, three things preceded the amphibious landings on August 15, 1944: an airdrop of almost 10,000 paratroopers to prepare the way for the infantry assault, an intense 90-minute aerial bombardment from 1,300 bombers, and a naval barrage. Battleship artillery pounded the German defenses as did rockets fired from smaller ships closer to shore. "Fired in batches, their missiles sail hissing through the air like schools of weird fish. They hit the earth, detonating mines, blasting barbed-wire entanglements, and unnerving the enemy," Murphy wrote. Underneath the canopy of rockets, the landing boats churned forward.[3]

Although this was the fourth beach assault carried out by the men of the 3rd Division, it was the first to unfold in daylight (H-hour was 0800) and the first in which Murphy came ashore in the first wave of attackers. As the boats closed in on the shoreline, Murphy stole glances at his fellow soldiers. He thought they looked "as miserable as wet cats." Many of the men were seasick. Murphy, for once, was not.

Their target was a beach labeled "Alpha Yellow," a two-mile long strip of sand just south of St. Tropez, and the landing was made "virtually without opposition, except from land mines." As Murphy carefully advanced across the sands, his eyes straining to pick up any glimmer of metal or telltale raised hump of sand, a mine exploded to his left killing the soldier who had stepped on it.

But as the first wave of troops came through, following soldiers had an easier time. "Thank God it was daylight," said one, because he could step directly into the footprints of previous soldiers.[4]

The attack had completely surprised the Germans who expected the Allies to come ashore much further to the east, and the 3rd Division easily seized the beachhead. Murphy and his company moved to clear out some of the more than 30,000 estimated German troops who held the "rocky pine-clad hills" that were immediately inland. An additional 200,000 German soldiers were estimated to be within a few days' march.

Murphy was ascending "Pill Box Hill" when he heard the crack of a rifle shot and saw the G.I. in front of him fall dead. Murphy hit the dirt as bullets zinged past him. He saw that if he rolled into an adjacent gully, he could continue up the hill, beneath the rifle fire, and find and take out the enemy. Staying low and moving fast, he rounded a slight bend in the ditch and came face to face with two German soldiers. In their shock they hesitated; Murphy did not, and killed them both. "When I get in a situation where it's tense and everything," he remarked later, "things seem to slow down for me. It doesn't seem a blur. Things become very clarified."[5]

The men he had killed had probably been looking for him, and in the meantime enemy fire kept pouring down. Murphy recognized he needed more firepower. He scurried down the hill, appropriated a light machine gun from a crew that was pinned down and refused to move, and then returned up the ditch, dragging the gun behind him, until he found a position where he target the German foxholes. He intended to take advantage of something he recognized instantly: because the Germans were firing downhill, at a depressed angle, their rifle stocks would be higher than their muzzles, and any German taking aim at him would have to expose his head, giving Murphy a chance of a shot. "I judge the range, press the trigger, and turn the stream of lead on anything that remotely resembles a kraut."

Scrambling quickly to the next foxhole—or even just a low spot in the ground—after each time he squeezed the trigger of his machine gun, he slowly worked his way up the hill. Before he reached the top he ran out of ammunition and, staying low, hurried back down the hill for more.

Lattie Tipton, bleeding profusely from a bullet that had hit him in the ear, finally caught up with Murphy at this point, and the two of them, taking turns covering each other, advanced, firing from the hip, and hurling grenades into enemy gun emplacements. Suddenly there was silence. Murphy and Tipton were crouched in a foxhole, their weapons trained on the next enemy emplacement. A German voice shouted "Kamerad!" Tipton warily stuck his head above the ground to take a look. "They're waving a handkerchief," he said with relief. "I'll go get them." Murphy urged him to stay down; the Germans could not be trusted. "You're getting to be a cynic," Tipton responded, standing up. A single shot from an unseen sniper hit him in the chest and sent him tumbling back into the hole atop his buddy. Murphy frantically tried to find a pulse while screaming for a medic—but, as Murphy, conceded, "I might as well be shouting at the moon, and the hill is rattling with fire."

"I never saw a drop of blood on him," Murphy said. "The sniper bullet must have got him in the heart." For the first time in the entire war, he later admitted, he refused to face facts, swearing that Tipton could not be dead. He counterattacked like a berserker, bursting from his foxhole firing his carbine. He killed the two Germans who had been shooting at him, grabbed their machine gun, and "holding it like a BAR for firing from the hip." Murphy found the gun crew that had killed Tipton and raked them with fire. "I remember the experience as I do a nightmare. A demon seems to have entered my body"— a demon that led him to clean out the entire hill of Germans. When the stress finally passed and the rush of adrenaline left his body, his hands began to tremble and he sank to the ground exhausted.[6]

The remainder of his company followed slowly in Murphy's wake, unsure if he were a hero or simply crazy. "Murph just lost his head," a buddy commented. "When you lose a buddy like that, it's really tough." When Murphy regained his feet he made his way back to his lifeless friend. He took Tipton's pack and placed it under the dead man's head as though it were a pillow, and then collapsed beside him, crying uncontrollably. It was the first and only time any of the other men in the company saw him cry. "In this tiny section of France the war is over," Murphy wrote later. "Above us white clouds float beneath a roof of pure blue. It is just another summer day." For his courage in taking the hill, Audie Murphy received the Distinguished Service Cross.

Murphy's ambivalence about being called a hero was a part of his being overtaken by a "demon" on the battlefield. Though he didn't know it, he was experiencing what the philosopher Aristotle had said long ago: there is a distinction between courageous action that comes from a conscious choice, motivated by reason and a striving after what is noble, and a beastlike ferocity born of emotional passion, pain, and a desire for revenge. Murphy felt the latter even if a dispassionate observer could attribute his actions solely to his high sense of duty, initiative, bravery, and martial skill.

In the future Murphy preferred to deflect attention from himself and deny that he was courageous—let alone a hero—partly because of his natural humility, but also because he understood that his courage was not something he consciously chose to do: it was nothing more than a natural reaction that did not seem overly praiseworthy to him and never would. In contrast, he instead bore a survivor's guilt over fighting men like Tipton, who gave all they had and never came home.

---

By nightfall of the first day, Murphy's 15th Regiment had accomplished all its goals and was assembling at the little village of Cogolin. Other soldiers from the 3rd Division entered the town of St. Tropez later in the afternoon only to find it already liberated by the French Forces of the Interior and hundreds of American paratroopers who, it turned out, had landed in the wrong place. The entire operation was proceeding far better than planners had dared expect. The Americans had suffered fewer than 500 casualties, and four-fifths of those were wounded. By the end of the second day of fighting, the lead units of the 3rd Division had pushed twenty miles inland into France in some places. Hoping to exploit the surprisingly weak German resistance, General Truscott ordered the 3rd and 45th Divisions to shift their attacks westward toward the port cities of Toulon and Marseilles and to the Rhone River Valley, a natural highway into the interior.

U.S. Army intelligence intercepted a general order to German troops in southern France to withdraw, which made resistance light and offered the opportunity of targeting German retreat routes. "We are receiving a great welcome in every town and village," one private with the 3rd Division wrote in his diary. "The people have had a pretty tough time under the Krauts." After the slow battering months in Italy, Murphy said, "our advance seems incredibly swift."[7]

But it didn't last. It wasn't the enemy that slowed them down now, but a shortage of trucks and gasoline. As it moved inland, a full corps of three American infantry divisions required about 100,000 gallons of fuel per day and while there was plenty of ammunition coming off the ships and piling up on the beaches, there was only about 11,000 gallons of gas in reserve. The shortages especially hampered efforts to send a task force racing up the Rhone Valley to the natural choke-point of the city of Montelimar with the intention of slowing or blocking the German escape. Faced with little other choice, on August 19, 1944, American generals made the painful decision to limit the northern and western advances of the army until Toulon and Marseilles fell. Fortunately for the Allies, by the end of August both ports had been liberated.

As they had done at Naples, however, the Germans had laid waste to the harbor facilities. Toulon, in fact, was so badly damaged that the Allies wrote it off as unusable. In Marseilles, there were thousands of mines strewn through the harbor along with sunken ships of every conceivable sort from the harbor's mouth all the way to the piers, where the Germans had also driven hundred of dock cranes into the water. Despite such destruction, American engineers went to work with alacrity and resolve and the first American Liberty ship pulled in to unload equipment and supplies on September 15. By contrast, the French rail network northward up the Rhone Valley was largely spared destruction, in part because Allied air power was then preoccupied with destroying rail infrastructure elsewhere.

The official U.S. Army history of the campaign notes that by the middle of September 1944, the German and the American armies that were flowing northward into central France were both more interested in getting to their desired positions—that is, linking up with other friendly forces operating in central France—as quickly as possible than they were in stopping or even slowing the other. It had become a race.

Audie Murphy's race would take his division north to Montelimar where the vanguard of advancing American forces had trapped a large contingent of German troops. Murphy's company initially bypassed the city in order to close in on it from the northeast and block any German units that might attempt to flee in that direction. One morning Murphy and his men spotted two German 88mm artillery pieces and a detachment of soldiers having breakfast. They crept in close and opened fire on the surprised Germans. Unable to lower the barrels of their big guns far enough to hit the approaching Americans directly, the Germans quickly switched to airburst shells, which showered them with deadly shrapnel. Murphy saw a German soldier with a rifle climb onto an artillery piece to get the advantage of elevation. "I see him as he lowers his rifle upon me and whip up my carbine." The two fired at the same time and the German's bullet hit the ground in front of Murphy so close it kicked dirt into his eyes. When he finally got his eyes open again, he saw the German dead on the ground, shot through the heart. Murphy dismissed it as a "lucky shot."[8]

Continuing forward and staying prone, Murphy suddenly saw the way to make a decisive breakthrough. Piles of 88mm artillery shells were stacked a short distance beyond the two big guns. He grabbed a bazooka from someone in his platoon, ordered the men to stay back, and crawled forward another fifty yards. When he judged the range to be correct, he sat up and quickly put three rounds into the stockpile. As it began to explode, the Germans leapt from their foxholes and fled, chased by American rifle fire. Murphy, leading his platoon forward, advanced rapidly and forced the Germans to surrender.

One of his next assignments was to lead a tedious and nerve-wracking house-to-house search for snipers in the city of Montelimar, while other elements from the 3rd and 36th Divisions caught a ten-mile-long convoy of 2,000 German vehicles trying to escape to the north. Artillery and air power reduced it to a smoldering mass of "dead soldiers, dead horses, and shattered enemy equipment." "The foul smell of burnt flesh was disgusting," remembered one of the men in Company B.[9]

After the fall of Montelimar, VI Corps continued north along the east bank of the Rhone, first to the city of Lyon seventy-five miles distant, then to Besancon, another 110 miles away. As they approached the Rhine, the plan was to link up with the right flank of General George S. Patton's Third Army, which was closing in from the west. American success had led some to call the campaign thus far the "Champagne campaign."[10]

The retreating German troops, however, had no intention of running all the way back to Germany. Their plan was to establish a formidable line extending northward from the Swiss border that would block the Americans from entering the Belfort Gap, a natural invasion route between the Vosges Mountains to the north and the Jura Mountains to the south. It was only fifteen miles wide at its narrowest point and led straight to the Rhine River and Germany. Meanwhile, the 3rd Division liberated Besancon on September 8, 1944, after two days of hard fighting, and captured 183,000 gallons of badly needed gas.

Murphy's platoon now became part of the rearguard of the American advance, but it was still in range of enemy fire. At a roadblock, in fact, his company came under a mortar attack, one shell hitting the ground directly in front of him. "It is practically under my feet before I am aware of it. I have just time enough to think, 'This is it,' before the blast knocks me unconscious." Murphy came to moments later, his broken carbine still clutched in his hands. His head ached and the air reeked of burned powder. As his eyes regained focus, he saw that a sergeant and a replacement with whom he had been talking moments before were dead, killed by the blast that had somehow—he had been closer to the explosion than they had been—only lacerated his foot and blown the heel off his boot. A few days later his sister received a telegram that he had been "slightly wounded in action."[11]

At the end of September Murphy returned from a short stay in the hospital just as the 3rd Division crossed the Moselle River and moved into the foothills of the Vosges Mountains. One of his buddies in Company B noted that most men from the hospital took several days to readjust. He could think of only two men who came back to duty "as calm and cool as ever under fire and combat conditions," and one was Audie Murphy.[12]

The going became slow and arduous in the rising, rocky country. The German retreat in front of Company B finally began to slow down and they more frequently turned to fight. Every day now "their resistance grows stronger, their retreats shorter." The terrain was perfect for defense, he said. Up the wooded hills Murphy and his men crept from tree to tree, boulder to boulder, knowing the Germans were just ahead in the silent trees that were now dripping from the constant autumn rains.[13]

Murphy's company now had as its objective the town of Le Tholy, which sat at the junction of two important roads. The German defenses were anchored by a stone quarry "so strategically located and fanatically defended that nothing short of a full-scale assault can eliminate it." It was also right in front of Company B.

The initial American attacks were driven back "with heavy losses by a hellish storm of enemy fire." Dead men lay scattered beneath the trees up to the edge of the quarry. By now, however, none of them was a buddy of Murphy's, simply because all his buddies were gone, returned stateside with a "million-dollar wound," as they were called, or killed in action. "I feel burnt out," Murphy said, "emotionally and physically exhausted. Let the hill be strewn with corpses so long as I do not have to turn over the bodies and find the familiar face of a friend."[14]

Battalion commander Lieutenant Colonel Michael Paulick led a recon patrol up the hill to assess the situation. Murphy watched them head out and then decided to trail along behind them. In his memoir, he said he was motivated by boredom more than anything else, and not wanting to be alone with his thoughts. Later he remarked to a friend that he went because he "figured those gentlemen were going to run into trouble."[15]

He was right, as usual. Up the hill under good cover a small detachment of eight Germans lay in wait. They opened fire on the patrol, catching it by surprise, and sent Paulick and his men scrambling for cover. The Germans didn't see Audie Murphy, who was trailing the patrol. Over the din of the shooting, Paulick heard Murphy yelling for him to stay down. One by one Murphy called each man's name and waited for a response. Paulick knew that he "must have some plan in mind and our position had something to do with it." Paulick had a high opinion of Murphy. He had noticed him back in Italy during the first battle of Cisterna and had considered him a born leader and potential officer material. His opinion was about to go even higher.

Stepping from behind a tree and throwing grenades while firing his carbine, Murphy killed four of the Germans and wounded the other four. Then he guided the wounded of the recon patrol back down the hill. He won a Silver Star for his action.[16]

Audie Murphy was far from done. Soon he was back up the hill after a sniper who had killed two men in the company's heavy weapons platoon. Murphy crept quietly through the tall trees, "the wooded hill a peaceful checkerboard of light and shade." Despite the tranquil appearance of the golden leaves and the shafts of dappled sunlight, the familiar cold hand of terror crept back into his body. He smacked his fist into his forehead to drive it away. He once again became the hunter of his youth, tracking a rabbit through the brush of Hunt County. A rustle of leaves. The snap of a twig. The barely perceptible movement of branches in a bush. Murphy dropped to one knee as he and the German sniper saw each other at the same moment. The hunter got off two shots before his prey could squeeze his trigger, hitting his target in the forehead twice. "I took my time on that one," Murphy later reflected coldly. "That sniper sonofabitch was lethal." His knees weak and queasiness rising, he made his way back down the hill to HQ to make his report. Then as he had done innumerable times since the days at Camp Wolters, he stripped his gun and began cleaning it.[17]

On October 3, 1944, two M-10 tank destroyers and two modified Sherman M4 tanks with larger guns were brought up to supplement an intense mortar barrage against the Germans entrenched in the quarry. The battalion fired a week's worth of rounds in a matter of hours. The tanks maneuvered to fire at point blank range. Two days later the remaining Germans abandoned the position and retreated down over the crest of the hill.

The Army's official history of the campaign noted that "Following the quarry fight, the 15th Infantry found the going easier as the Germans grudgingly gave way." Murphy's own account is a little different. The ordeal for his company was not yet over. Contrary to their usual tactic, the Germans had dug in along a streambed at the bottom of the hill, and their machine guns tore at the men of Company B from perfect camouflage as they came down. By nightfall of the next day, they were pinned down again.[18]

Dragging a radio behind him, Murphy moved "like a lizard" down the hill. Later he said he was so cold and scared that he was afraid his chattering teeth would give away his position. Bullets hit the ground around him, as close as a foot away, but somehow they missed. He spotted the shape of a German helmet poking up above a log and froze, waiting for it to rise. It started moving. When he saw the white flash of bare forehead, he fired. "The head snaps backwards as if caught in a hangman's noose." He scrambled for his radio, checked his map, and called in a mortar attack on where the Germans were dug in. In what seemed like one single movement he dropped his radio, grabbed his carbine and fired as a German soldier peered around a tree just up ahead. Murphy's shot hit him in the throat. He picked up his radio again and kept calling in fire until finally the mortars found their target. He kept this up for an entire hour. Fifteen enemy soldiers were killed and thirty-five wounded. "The game of hide-and-go-seek is over for the Germans," Murphy said. He won another award for valor for this action.[19]

The weather turned colder as the company paused to rest and reorganize. Frost lay on the ground in the mornings and off to the north the men could see snow on the peaks of the Vosges. At night they shivered as they tried to sleep. Murphy and two other men were called to regimental HQ one cold night to discover they had all been promoted to second lieutenant. He had refused such a promotion once before, in Italy, in part because of his lack of much formal education, about which he was very self-conscious, and partly because he knew it was common practice to move promoted officers away from the units through which they had come up. Understanding that Murphy was extremely loyal to the men around him, his battalion commander had already obtained a waiver for him to remain with his unit despite his promotion—thus Murphy became Second Lieutenant Audie L. Murphy. The rank was thought of by many enlisted men as something of a death sentence because it was common knowledge that second lieutenants had the highest casualty rate of any officer in World War II. Over one particularly tough period of fighting in Italy, the 3rd Division experienced a casualty rate of 152 percent among second lieutenants. The two other men commissioned with Murphy that night would be killed in action before the war was over.

The Vosges campaign became a numbing slog up one forested hillside and down another. Meanwhile, stories of Audie Murphy's nerve, aim, and bravery spread through the ranks of the 3rd Division. Long before his name became known outside the Army, soldiers in his division knew it well. After the war a former artilleryman with the 3rd was asked if Murphy had been well known before his fame. "Lord, yes!" he said. "I don't suppose there was a real veteran in the whole division who was not aware of him. If Murphy was in the front lines, we in the rear area went to sleep." And if he ever started retreating, they knew "it was time to clear out and fast." His buddies in Company B began to call him "Blood and Guts, Jr." after the officer whom everyone referred to as "Old Blood and Guts," General George S. Patton.[20]

On October 17, 1944, Murphy's regiment came out of the front lines for three days of rest and training. The 3rd Division's commander, Major General John O'Daniel (whose nickname was nevertheless "Iron Mike") believed that there had been a noticeable decline in the aggressiveness of some of his men. The replacements coming in were poorly trained, often inept. Aside from the effects of unrelenting combat, all his men were constantly cold and wet and tired, but he insisted to his subordinates that going easy on the troops would only prolong the war and make things harder in the end. By contrast, General John Dahlquist, the commander of the 36th Division, which had been fighting alongside the 3rd since the beaches of Provence, established little rest camps for his troops through which they constantly rotated. "You give them three days" of rest, he said, "and they'll... be back in shape without any trouble. Just leave them alone, let them sleep and eat the first day, make them clean up the second day, and do whatever they want to the rest of the time, and they'll be ready to go."[21]

The rain continued. "It sure is nasty weather over here now," Audie Murphy wrote to Mrs. Cawthon back in Celeste, whom he still called "Mom." The cold continued as well, as did the constant threat from German snipers that seemed to lurk behind every rock and tree. Murphy bagged a sniper's rifle from one of the snipers he killed. He kept it through the remainder of the war and long after.

Besides snipers, artillery barrages were the other regularly terrifying occurrence, high explosive shells bursting in the trees above the Americans, mixing metal shrapnel with splintered tree limbs that were like spears hurtling downward.

The 3rd Division went back into the lines on October 20, 1944. Six days later, Murphy and his platoon radio operator were advancing cautiously, side by side, following a moving artillery barrage through the forest. A German sniper got them in his sights, and with his first shot he hit the radioman above his left eye, sending him sprawling backward. Murphy dove for cover. The sniper's second shot caromed off a tree and hit Murphy in the right hip and buttock. A platoon sergeant heard Murphy say, "I'll be damned, I've been shot right in the ass."[22]

Keeping hold of his carbine, Murphy watched until the sniper revealed his position, abruptly throwing off his camouflage cape to get a better shot. When he fired again it inexplicably hit Murphy's helmet which was several feet from where he was lying wounded. It was all the chance Murphy needed. His return shot hit the sniper squarely between the eyes. Murphy tried to get up but his right leg would not respond and he slumped back to the ground as a soldier from his platoon ran up to check on him. His wound was long and deep but thankfully the bullet had passed through him and missed the bone, though it felt like "white-hot brand had been raked across" the gash. His men helped Murphy back to the road where he was put on a stretcher across the hood of a jeep, which then bounced its way back to the battalion aid station.

CHAPTER SIX

# A WEARY VICTOR

Second Lieutenant Audie Murphy lay on one of six cots, listening to the pitter-patter of rain hitting the canvas above his head. He was still at the battalion aid station. The roads leading to the rear were little more than rivers of mud, and he was stuck here. He was not impressed. The first medic who examined him, looked to Murphy "as if he had never seen a wounded man before." "Goddammit, do *something*," Murphy muttered. But there was little the medics could do at the aid station except keep the men quiet, kill pain with morphine, and wait for the roads to become passable so that the men could be transferred to a hospital. Three days passed. Murphy's fever rose.[1]

Finally he was transferred to the Army's Third General Hospital in Aix-en-Provence, near Marseilles. There the doctor's diagnosis at last confirmed what Murphy himself had come to suspect. His untreated wound had developed gangrene, a harrowing condition in which infected flesh simply blackens and dies. The only treatment available at the time was penicillin, but because it could not penetrate the dead tissue in which the blood was stagnant those areas had to be cut away. For a limb this would mean amputation, and had Audie Murphy developed the condition in his arm or leg, it would have been the end of his military career. But for gangrene in the buttocks, a simple amputation was not an option. They gave him penicillin every three hours and continually cut away the dead parts of his flesh—in all, five pounds of it. His treatment would keep him in the hospital for more than two months.

His fame in the division was spreading and many staffers at the hospital knew his name by the time he arrived. But few could reconcile the tales of battlefield valor with the boyish young man they were treating. "[I]f I had to choose a candidate for the 'The Great American War Hero' from that ward of officers," one nurse said, "Murph would have been at the bottom of the list." "He looked like a high school kid," said one of the other soldiers there getting treatment. "I was amazed how small he was." He was charming, and the nurses, at least, found him nearly irresistible. One of the nurses had her first glimpse of him in the hospital kitchen licking a mixing spoon that had just been used to stir a batch of fudge. He "had the fresh boyish freckled face of a high school sophomore," one of them later said. Another nurse described him as "someone you wanted to hug and take home with you." "Don't let that baby face fool you," an officer told her, "that's the toughest soldier in the 3rd Division."[2]

He became particularly close with an attractive twenty-four-year-old lieutenant in the Army Nurse Corps named Carolyn Price. She worked the overnight shift in the ward where Murphy was, and they got to know each other very well. He suffered from insomnia, and after lights-out he would get out of bed and come down to the nurse's station where he would read, visit with the ward men, and wait for

Price to finish her work so he could talk to her. He was, for the most part, a good and compliant patient from her perspective. He did not horse around or tell dirty jokes with the other soldiers. But he caused trouble of a different sort. "He was difficult to convince that he should follow doctor's orders," she said. He blithely disregarded the surgeon's insistence that unless he stayed in bed his infection would never heal.[3]

Murphy opened up to Carolyn Price to a surprising degree, given how taciturn he could be around most people. It is quite likely that he fell in love with her, or something very close to it, which was certainly not an unheard of reaction between a soldier in the hospital and his nurse. He was, after all, only nineteen years old. He told her stories about his family back in Texas, his sisters and brothers, especially his younger siblings whom he vowed anew to get out of the orphanage as soon as he returned to Hunt County. He told her, however, that while he wanted to go back to get them out of the orphanage he had no intention of returning to the kind of life he had known before the war. He confessed that at times he had even thought he would become some sort of mercenary soldier. After all, it was now what he knew best. It horrified her. She noticed that the only thing he would not talk about was his combat experience. "This seemed to be a part of his life he could share with no one." He did tell her, over and over, that he wanted to get back to the front and to the men of his platoon. Every single day he asked how long it would be before he could return to duty.

Also while he was in the hospital, Murphy met a critically wounded soldier named Perry Pitt who recently had been told by the doctors that he would be a paraplegic for the rest of his life. He was taking it hard. The nurse classified Pitt as "a non-sleeper" like Murphy, and sometimes at night he would softly call Murphy over. Murphy spent hours at Pitt's bedside talking with him and encouraging him. The two became life-long friends.

Finally Murphy was well enough to be discharged from the hospital. He was transferred to a convalescent camp a few miles outside of town. When he felt up to it, he would catch a ride into Aix-en-Provence and he and Price would have a date, dining at the officer's mess when she got off duty, and walking her to her quarters afterwards. One afternoon they went to a small bistro in Aix-en-Provence. From their corner booth, they overheard soldiers drinking at the bar commenting loudly about a newly minted "baby-faced" officer getting to go out on a date with a pretty nurse. Murphy's "face became grim and white, his eyes grew cold and narrow," and Price feared there might be a fight. She talked him out of it, and they left quickly.

Murphy's infatuation with Carolyn Price culminated in his proposing marriage, which she gracefully deflected. He continued to write her letters from the front. He might be a hardened veteran, but he had a romantic nature too. "He was always falling desperately in love with some girl," a friend said after the war.

Audie Murphy was discharged from the convalescent camp on December 29, 1944. His gruesome infection was gone, but for the rest of his life he carried a nine-inch scar as a memento of it. After his discharge, the Army officially classified him as 50 percent disabled, mostly because of this episode.

------

Two weeks before he was discharged, the German army staged a last desperate offensive through the Ardennes Forest that caught the American Army entirely by surprise. It became known as "The Battle of the Bulge," so named for the tremendous westward bulge that the attack had created in the Allied lines in southern Belgium.

Meanwhile, to the south the 3rd Division had finally broken through the Vosges Mountains. Some soldiers who had experienced the hell at Anzio ranked the fighting in the Vosges as even tougher. On Thanksgiving Day, French and American troops rolled into the city of Strasbourg on the Rhine River. The Seventh Army (of which the 3rd Division was a part) was now poised to break into Germany, but was halted by Supreme Allied Commander General Dwight Eisenhower who wanted its divisions available to support units in the north. Further to the south, west of the Rhine the Germans held an 850-square-mile bulge, which, if not as immediately threatening as the surprise German offensive in Belgium, was nevertheless, as Audie Murphy described it, "a huge and dangerous bridgehead thrusting west of the Rhine like an iron fist." At the top of the fist was the French city of Colmar, which gave its name to the salient: The Colmar Pocket. It "makes our position a precarious one," Eisenhower remarked. "[U]ntil we get firmly established on the Rhine," he said, "we are not in position to make the attack which we hope will be fatal to the other fellow."[4]

German commanders saw that launching an offensive in the south could simultaneously take advantage of the Allies' focus on the Battle of the Bulge and relieve some of the pressure on German troops there. On the night of December 31, 1944, German troops attacked north of Strasbourg in an operation called "Nordwind," with a coordinating attack planned to come out of the Colmar Pocket codenamed "Sonnenwende."

---

Murphy was still on rehab leave when the German offensive opened. He did not rejoin his company until January 14, 1945, and his buddies were shocked at his condition. He even had to be helped to take his shoes and socks off. But whatever Murphy's condition, in the opinion of the dogface soldiers, "we would have been ashamed not to follow" him.[5]

The 15th Regiment had been in action at the Colmar Pocket from the beginning of the German offensive and had not given way. Now it was to counterattack. Allied intelligence calculated there were six to nine German divisions—as many as 50,000 troops—within the pocket. "Each Alsatian hamlet and crossroads had become a defensive strongpoint." Ahead lay what Murphy called one of the toughest assignments in the history of the 3rd Division.[6]

The attack began on January 20, 1945, and in three days the 30th Regiment cleared the Riedwihr Forest and reached the little twin towns of Holtzwihr and Riedwihr. There, however, the regiment ran into ten enemy tanks and hundreds of infantry. The 30th had no tanks and could not even dig foxholes in the frozen ground. By the end of the day they had to fall back through the forest. Murphy's regiment, which had been held in reserve, moved into action the next day. The result was largely the same: the men driven back in disarray. "We looked like a flock of scared sheep running across the field as fast as our legs would carry us," said one of the men in the regiment.[7]

It was clear that without some sort of armor—either tanks or tank destroyers—the infantry would not be able to make any progress. It was bitterly cold. That night as he slept, Murphy's hair froze to the ground and he lost some of it when he jerked awake at the sound of gunfire. On the morning of January 25, 1945, the regiment was reinforced with armored units and advanced into the forest. Murphy was wounded by a German mortar barrage that killed the two second lieutenants who had been commissioned with him. Murphy's legs were cut by innumerable small metal fragments. His wounds were not serious enough to send him back to the aid station, but they did result in his receiving a second Oak Leaf Cluster on his Purple Heart, signifying his three times being wounded in battle.

Early in the small hours of the next morning, January 26, Murphy was summoned to regimental headquarters and given command of Company B because its first lieutenant had been badly wounded. Murphy led the company into action that morning, moving out of the forest toward the small village of Holtzwihr. Around dawn on another grey and overcast morning, two M10 tank destroyers squeaked and lumbered into position to support the infantry attack. Murphy had his carbine, a map, a pair of binoculars and a telephone that was connected to the battalion headquarters, about a mile behind where his attack was to kick off. Advancing out of the woods along a small dirt road, the men of Company B could see the village in the distance. Murphy set up his command post in a shallow drainage ditch that meandered along the right side of the road; he had tank destroyers on either side of ditch, one about forty yards ahead, the other about ten yards to his rear.

Early in the afternoon, battalion headquarters told Murphy to hold his position and wait for the 30th Regiment to come up as his reserve. Murphy peered through his binoculars at the little village just about a mile away, knowing the Germans were there, expecting them to come out at any moment. At 1400—that is, 2:00 in the afternoon—they finally did. From a shallow foxhole at the front of his company's position, Murphy saw six tanks in two groups of three moving in an obvious attempt to flank his position. Then he saw the soldiers, "wave after wave of white dots," maybe 250 of them, dressed in their white winter gear, making them "barely discernable against the backdrop of snow." Unlike the troops, the German tanks were highly visible, right down to the little pennants fluttering on the end of their antennae in the cold wind. Murphy scrambled back to his command post, grabbed the field telephone, and gave the enemy coordinates to battalion artillery control. At that moment "all hell broke loose," he said, as an artillery and mortar barrage erupted from German guns in and around the town.

Murphy knew he had to hold this road, which led to the 15th Regiment's headquarters. As the Germans advanced, Murphy called in updated map coordinates for artillery fire. He quickly discovered that the shells from his tank destroyers were simply not strong enough to disable the heavy German Tiger tanks; even direct hits did not slow them. Instead, the Tigers took out the forward American machine gun position and then demolished the tank destroyer behind him, killing its commander and gunner. Amidst the swirling black smoke, Murphy turned to see the other members of the crew scramble out and flee.

To his front, the crew of the other tank destroyer had given up trying to take out the German tanks and instead its crew was directing its .50 and .30 caliber machine gun fire at the advancing infantry. But as its driver tried to maneuver it into a better position, it slid into the ditch, its guns at an angle that made it impossible to fire.

Finally the American artillery slammed into the battlefield. "Our counterbarrage is on the nose," Murphy said. Advancing German infantrymen vanished in clouds of smoke and snow. But more continued to close the distance to the Americans. Then the tanks were close enough to use their machine guns. Murphy thought the situation was hopeless. He yelled for his men to withdraw, but, for himself, was determined to stay on the phone and direct the American artillery. The closest Germans were now only about 200 yards away. "Get the hell out of here," he yelled when he saw the men hesitating. He grabbed his carbine. "That's an order!" Murphy reasoned "that if one man,"—himself—"could do the job, why risk the lives of others?"

The Germans kept coming "on and on as though nothing would stop them." Murphy scrambled back to the .50 caliber machine gun mounted atop the burning tank destroyer to his rear. He did not know if the gun was still operable, but it was now the only chance he had to slow down the Germans. He dragged the phone over to it and climbed on top. The body of the lieutenant was half in and half out of the turret, his blood running down the side. Murphy pulled him the rest of the way out and dumped him to the ground. He stood up and checked the gun, found it was not damaged at all, and pulled the bolt back. When he squeezed the trigger "the chatter of the gun is like sweet music. Three krauts stagger and crumple in the snow." He swept the gun across his field of fire, peering through the swirling smoke searching for more targets. He "killed them in the draws, in the meadows, in the woods—wherever he saw them," one eyewitness said later. Murphy knew that the German tanks would break off their advance if they had no infantry to accompany them, so he tried to take out as many soldiers as he could. The artillery phone continued to ring. "How close are they to your position?" came the frantic voice. "Just hold the phone and I'll let you talk to one of the bastards," Murphy shouted back, in a retort that would soon become famous.[8]

There was a thunderous crash as the tank destroyer shook from not one but two direct hits. Murphy swayed but regained his balance and, still holding onto the map, kept yelling coordinates into the telephone. The American artillerymen adjusted their fire closer and closer to his position. He grabbed another belt of ammo and jammed it into the feeder. The smoke was so thick that he could barely see through it, but then a gust of wind broke it up just long enough to give him a clear view of his targets. In the smoke and chaos of battle Murphy guessed that the Germans "probably didn't even hear my machine gun fire, much less guess its point of origin." They only knew they were being mowed down. "For the time being my imagination is gone; and my numbed brain is intent only on destroying. I am conscious only that the smoke and the turret afford a good screen." Later he would add with characteristic humor that standing atop the blazing, disabled machine with the Germans closing in was the first time his feet had been warm in days.

Another gust of wind blew the smoke away and he spied a squad of Germans over in the ditch, a mere thirty yards from where he was. Before he could spin and fire, another billow of smoke obscured them. In the next break he caught them and left all twelve slumped in a pile. For good measure he swept the gun back over the bodies and unloaded more bullets into them. Then there came an explosion of a different sort. An American shell landed only fifty yards away followed by an enemy shell that landed even closer, stunning Murphy and nearly knocking him from his perch. Smoke belched from the burning vehicle beneath him. One soldier who saw the action expected "to see the whole damn tank destroyer blow up under him any minute." Murphy shouted new coordinates into the telephone, but there was no answer. The last round of German artillery had cut the line. Then he noticed the attacking soldiers were falling back. The German tanks had broken off the attack.[9]

The map clutched in Murphy's hand was tattered from shell fragments. His right leg throbbed in pain and he blandly noticed that his pant leg was soaked with blood. He slid down off the tank and started walking to the rear. The battle was over. "Existence has taken on the quality of a dream in which I am detached from all that is present." Shortly, his legs started shaking and he leaned against a tree, feeling his adrenaline subside and the familiar aching weariness returning to his body. It was then that he heard the welcome sound of American aircraft roaring over the battlefield. He looked up to see that the morning overcast had broken. Suddenly there was a thunderous blast as the tank destroyer on which he had been standing exploded, its turret and machine gun blown into the woods.

Those who were witnesses to Audie Murphy's feat were incredulous at what had transpired. Some could barely believe what they had seen. "He saved our lives," said one soldier from Company B. "If he hadn't done what he did, the Germans would have annihilated us." It was, said a lieutenant who was one of the forward artillery observers, "the bravest thing I've ever seen a man do in combat." For the rest of the day, the company held its position, wary of a renewed attack that did not come. The 30th regiment finally arrived. The next day, American troops took Holtzwihr.[10]

The operation to reduce the Colmar Pocket proceeded apace, and "in one brief but brutal assault after another" they pushed the enemy from their sector of the map. Replacements arrived; wounded and broken men were sent to the rear. By January 28, 1945, the Americans had cleared out most of the German troops from the north side of the Colmar Canal, a fifty-foot wide channel with twelve-foot-high banks that connected the city with the Rhine River. The following night Murphy's regiment led the crossing of the canal, meeting minimal German resistance.[11]

Company B moved faster now, liberating villages and towns, and accepting the surrender of German troops who sometimes outnumbered their captors. The Americans bypassed the German strongpoint of Colmar itself and instead cut it off from resupply and reinforcements.

One night, the company received orders to push on double-quick to capture a bridge over another canal—a bridge that American commanders worried the Germans would blow up. As Murphy roused his exhausted men, an artillery barrage slammed into their position, killing eight soldiers. One man cracked up under the stress. It was not his fault, Murphy said later. "He has courage to spare, but body and nerves have taken all they can stand. He has heard one explosion too many; seen one man too many die." The man was not alone. From August 15 through the end of the year there were 10,000 psychiatric cases diagnosed in the Seventh Army, and only one-third of them returned to duty. The rapidity of the army's advance put added strain on combat commanders at all levels. "Sleep is not among our rations," he commented. Murphy's attitude had changed markedly from his days on Sicily when he regarded such men with contempt and disgust. He himself had now seen too many explosions and too much death to know the toll that such experiences could take on one's mind and nerves.[12]

During their advance Company B captured a group of apparently exhausted Germans soldiers. They surrendered and tossed their helmets to the ground, slumping with their heads in their hands. Shortly after, three German tanks emerged from the neighboring woods accompanied by a handful of soldiers. Thinking quickly, Murphy and his men put on the German helmets and waved at the tanks, a mere thirty yards away. "For the next ten minutes, I scarcely breathe. If one prisoner shouts, if one German eye examines the dirty uniforms beneath our helmets, it is the end for us." But Murphy's ruse worked, and he and his men survived, the tanks passing harmlessly by.

After the Colmar Pocket was cleared, the exhausted men of the 3rd Division were pulled from the front lines and sent to a rest camp near the city of Nancy. In seven grueling weeks of fighting the division had suffered more than 4,500 casualties.

————————

Murphy took advantage of this break in the fighting to visit Paris, which he did at least twice. He liked it better than Rome, or at least he did not complain about it in the same way. He also bought some fancy French perfume for his sister.

With victory nearly in sight, some soldiers talked about going home. But Murphy took no part in it. "I have seen too much to be optimistic," he said. Every mile of whatever kind of offensive was coming next "must be bought with somebody's blood. Why not mine?" Even his battalion commander noticed the "almost fatalistic view of life and combat" he had developed. "Somewhere, sometime, the bullet bearing my name will find me."[13]

While in Nancy, Murphy was promoted to First Lieutenant, received his Distinguished Service Cross and a Silver Star, and heard that he would be awarded the Medal of Honor. He wrote his sister "Boy if I get that I will soon be comeing [sic] home." Each medal contributed five points toward a discharge from the Army. He was also in line to receive the French Legion of Merit.

At the end of February 1945, units of the 3rd Division began training for urban combat. It underlined for Murphy the hard fighting they might still face in Germany. "So until the last shot is fired, I will go on living day to day, making no postwar plans."

But when Company B of the 15th Regiment of the 3rd Division returned to action against the "Siegfried Line," Germany's western fortifications, Audie Murphy was no longer there. He was now a regimental liaison officer. It was standard procedure, one colonel explained, that when someone in an infantry company was recommended for the Medal of Honor he was automatically taken out of his unit and assigned to "the relative safety of regimental headquarters." Murphy's job was to maintain communication between the division's units. He was given a jeep (with a .50 caliber machine gun mounted in the rear), a driver, and an interpreter. It was an important assignment, but he was deeply disappointed by it. As he had said repeatedly, he wanted to be with his company, with the fighting men.[14]

Liaison officers were still exposed to periodic danger as they moved between units, particularly when the officer was as determined to be on the front lines as was Audie Murphy. At one point he got word that two of Company B's officers had been killed and the rest of the company was pinned down in a deserted enemy trench somewhere near the Siegfried Line. "For two days I brooded over the news while running official errands in the rear," he said. "But finally I could take it no longer." The company was part of his life's blood, he said. He located their spot on a map and with the alibi that he was going to check on a telephone line, went to the company's position, ordering his driver to stay in the jeep once they arrived. The demoralized troops suddenly saw him calmly walking toward them, carbine in hand. He paced the line exhorting the men to get up and move forward. They emerged from their trenches, looking dazed. It looked to Murphy "like a mass collapse of nerves. I would like to pull them back for a rest, but I cannot. They have to move forward." No one fired a shot at them as the men advanced behind their leader. He maneuvered them into a place where they would be contacted by other units. When Murphy returned to headquarters he discovered that no one had even realized he had been gone.[15]

In Murphy's sector it seemed that the push into Germany had become "like a great river pushing against a series of rotting dams." "We are moving so fast lately that I don't hardly have time to stop for chow," he wrote his sister. Sometimes just locating the front became a challenge. Once when he was on patrol, Murphy crept up to a German unit and noted that "A hand grenade could have wiped out the lot of them." The Germans looked just like Americans, he thought, "gabbing, horsing around, eating their rations peacefully." Hitler was using ever younger soldiers to fill the ranks of his army, and it bothered Murphy when he came across them. Let them live, he decided. He pulled back silently, leaving them alone. Later, he characterized his actions as "turning chicken."[16]

After the Americans captured a town, Audie Murphy usually followed close behind in a jeep. The scenes were all similar. White flags made from bed sheets fluttered from windows. Cities that had been pummeled first by bombs and then later by artillery were now shapeless piles of ruin. The "picture of mass defeat," he said, was "the most awesome spectacle of the war." Witnessing the endless columns of beaten German soldiers streaming past him toward POW camps, it was impossible to see in these men the existential threat they had posed to him and to his buddies just a short time before. Day by day the end of the war in Europe grew closer. On April 21, 1945, the men of the 3rd Division saw the American flag raised over the city of Nuremburg. On May 5 they saw it raised over Salzburg. Walking the streets of the historic city in which Mozart had been born, Murphy spotted a German colonel still wearing his pistol. He brusquely demanded the man hand it over. After a tense few seconds, he did. Years later Murphy was asked what he would have done if the officer had refused. "I would have killed the S.O.B.," he said simply.[17]

The 3rd Division was sent to garrison the small town of Werfen, thirty-five miles south of Salzburg, and the site of a German Officer Candidate School. Murphy was granted leave and returned to France. He was in Lyon when he heard voices shouting, chanting, and singing outside his hotel window. People were dancing in the street. The war was officially over. "My blood pressure went way down and stayed there." Slowly the indescribable weariness settled in. It would never leave.

# CHAPTER SEVEN

# A HERO RETURNS TO TEXAS

udie Murphy slid down into a hot bath, luxuriating in the alien feeling of cleanliness and warmth. He felt his muscles relax. His eyes, that had seen so much that was unspeakable, began to droop. He was in a hotel room in Cannes, France, along with a young lieutenant who had shared his compartment on the train, and who at this moment was shaving and preparing to go out on the town. "You want to come along?" he asked. Murphy did not. He wanted a nap.[1]

When he awoke some time later in his quiet room, he began dressing. As he searched through his pack for his necktie, he picked up his service pistol. It felt good and reassuring in his hand. For years it had represented security, a last line of defense. Now "it is more beautiful than a flower; more faithful than most friends." A pistol would always be a source of comfort for Murphy. He was at ease with guns, had loved them since his boyhood, and did in fact find them "more faithful than most friends." Somewhere from close by a church bell started ringing. He grabbed his tie and went out into the town.

The streets were crowded, overflowing with revelers, jubilation at every turn with the official end of the war. But as he pressed through the people, he was not happy. Instead, he was irritated. In the middle of the crowd, he was lonely. In the middle of the celebration, he felt uneasy. "I want company, and I want to be alone. I want to talk, and I want to be silent. I want to sit, and I want to walk. There is VE-Day without, but no peace within." His memories of the previous years pushed aside the party. The uproar of the festivities all around him was abruptly replaced in his imagination by the uproar of combat, the exulting faces by those of his dying comrades. He finally had to retreat to his room. Now, however, he could not sleep.

"One day the war is over," Murphy wrote years later reflecting on that day. "The men, with their twisted brains and shattered nerves; with a hard vision for truth and [an] impatience with stupidity, take off their uniforms. But the military, which has so carefully, systematically, and gradually changed them into soldiers, does nothing to reverse the process. Perhaps it could not. The scars are too deep." Even though the war had just ended, Murphy felt those scars already.[2]

One afternoon as he was walking the promenade along the beach, he saw a familiar face. It was Henry Bodson, the officer who had taught him artillery spotting in Italy and whom he had run into occasionally in subsequent months. "He seemed real glad to see me," Bodson later said, "and was much more talkative than I had known him to be." The two spent a lot of time together, talking about their experiences and the "great events of the war." When they finally grew tired of walking, Murphy invited Bodson to his hotel room for a drink where their conversation turned toward their postwar hopes and plans. The uncertainty of the future was weighing heavily on Audie Murphy. They spoke of the Army as being a potential career path for him and of the chances of him going to the U.S. Military Academy at West Point. Finally they said their good-byes and parted ways. Murphy was "open, fair, honest, and forthright; there was nothing phony about him. And he had a bit of a mean Texas streak that occasionally showed," Bodson added.[3]

The chance encounter had been a thoroughly welcome distraction for Murphy, but he was soon lonely and unsettled again. He telephoned the hospital in Aix-en-Provence to talk to Carolyn Price. He hoped that she could come to Cannes for a few days for a visit. She thought he sounded "lonely, bored, and unhappy," but told him she was much too busy to get away. A few days later, the ward master at the hospital came to her to say there was a young officer asking to see her. It was Audie Murphy.[4]

When her shift ended the two had dinner together in the officers' mess at the hospital. No longer was he an anonymous patient. Their conversation was repeatedly interrupted by officers and doctors introducing themselves and congratulating him on his awards. He had, Price said, so many ribbons and medals, he looked like Army Chief of Staff George Marshall (although he had yet to receive the Medal of Honor, the French Legion of Honor, and some others). He seemed pleased at the attention but also a little embarrassed. Price later wrote to their mutual friend Perry Pitt, "He's dreadfully tired. I do wish he'd accept a discharge."

---

Some of Murphy's commanding officers were thinking in exactly the opposite direction. The Commanding Officer of the 3rd Division, Major General John W. O'Daniel, personally inquired about whether Audie Murphy would be eligible to attend the U.S. Military Academy at West Point that coming fall. Murphy's character, he reported to the Supreme Headquarters of the Allied Expeditionary Force, was excellent, he met the physical requirements, and he had "demonstrated positively outstanding ability for leadership." He knew the entrance regulations at West Point pertained to enlisted men only, but he hoped that an exception could be made for Murphy who, after all, was already an "outstanding" officer.

It was inadvisable, came the reply a few days later, because of the time available for Murphy to prepare for the entrance exam. But "in any event, he should be favorably considered for a regular army commission," and, if Congress changed the age requirements for admission—and the requirement for a physical exam could in his case be waived—it was possible that Murphy could join a program called the USMA Preparatory Unit in the 1945–46 academic year.

In fact, the idea of Murphy attending West Point was a nonstarter. One of his biographers, Harold Simpson, himself a retired Army officer, believed that Audie Murphy's desire to attend the United States Military Academy "was really an impossible dream. It would have taken too much concentrated study to make up the deficit in his education in order to have qualified for entry into either" West Point or into Texas A&M, another school in which he had expressed an interest. It is easy to forget in light of his other abilities that Audie Murphy had only a fifth grade education. Such a disadvantage could not be easily overcome by anyone.[5]

On May 20, 1944, he returned to Werfen and command of Company B. A few days later, the War Department officially announced that Murphy had won the Congressional Medal of Honor for his action around Holtzwihr. The medal ceremony was set for June 2, 1945, at an airfield near Salzburg.

Nine U.S. Senators from the Senate Military Affairs committee were on hand for the ceremony, including Harry Byrd of West Virginia, Richard Russell of Georgia, and James Eastland of Mississippi.

Since it was now safe to fly in and out of Europe, that morning the group had flown into Salzburg to tour Hitler's nearby mountain retreat.

As General Alexander Patch, Commander of the U.S. Seventh Army, put the blue ribbon of the award around Murphy's neck he quietly asked him, "Are you as nervous as I am?" "Yes sir," Murphy answered with tears in his eyes, "I'm afraid I am." Patch then pinned the Legion of Merit onto Murphy's uniform. Audie Murphy was now the most decorated soldier in American history, and he would later receive additional awards from France and Belgium. It was estimated that he had killed 240 enemy soldiers in about twenty months of combat.

After the ceremony, Murphy returned to regimental headquarters at Werfen Castle, where he posed with his new medals for photographers. In the pictures, Murphy tried to appear stern-faced, but the young boy keeps peeking through; he looks hardly older than he did as a gas station attendant in Greenville.

Audie Murphy now had a choice: he could remain in Europe as part of the postwar occupation force, and most likely be promoted to captain, or he could return to the states on rest leave. He chose Texas. He wanted to go home.

Even before he left Europe he was well on his way to being enshrined as a hero in his home state. On June 1, 1945, the Texas legislature passed a resolution honoring him. By his bravery and determination to win, the legislators gushed, "he has handed down to all Texas the glory and courage that has made Texas soldiers the greatest fighters in the world." He was a "very splendid young soldier" and a "gallant and courageous young Texan." Audie Murphy had no way of realizing it, but he was becoming the talk of the state. Two days later the *Houston Chronicle* reported that "Young Murphy" would be coming home to Texas soon, "and says he will use the back doors 'because I don't go for this hero stuff.'" As he would discover, the choice would not be his to make.

———

On June 10, Audie Murphy flew out of Salzburg bound for Paris. From there he flew to the Azores, then to a base in Maine, then to Houston where he and the group travelling with him—thirteen generals, including Alexander Patch and Lucian Truscott, and forty-five other officers and enlisted men with multiple citations for valor—spent their last night in transit. Flying to their final destination of San Antonio, their three C-54 Army Air Corps transport planes were met in the air by an incredible escort fleet of eighty fighters and bombers. After they landed and taxied up to the cheering crowds, flashbulbs popped as one by one the soldiers came down the stairs from the planes. Audie Murphy was the last one off his plane. As he went through the reception line at the airport, shaking hands and smiling shyly, he was shocked to discover that everyone seemed to recognize him.

"Stars fell on San Antonio," enthused the *Dallas Morning News* in trying to convey the sprawling scene to its readers. There was a huge parade that meandered from the airport to downtown with as many as 300,000 people jammed along the route. In honor of the visitors all the stores downtown were closed for the day. Flowers rained down on the open cars as they passed through the cheering crowds, some tossed by spectators perched on building rooftops to get a better look. Many of the officers and men teared up at the intensity and sincerity of the welcome. Of all the heroes being celebrated, none embodied the image that people wanted to see more than Audie Murphy: humble, boyish, and still innocent-looking, yet courageous beyond measure.

The parade ended at the opulent St. Anthony Hotel where a reception and a press conference were scheduled for the afternoon. That night, Murphy was scheduled to be guest of honor at a dinner a few blocks away, where the mayor would introduce him as the most decorated soldier in American history, the first time he would be so described in public. The introduction was made, and the mayor and the diners craned their necks to spot him, but Murphy was not there and never appeared at the dinner at all. Back at the hotel he had struck up a conversation with a pretty young elevator attendant and invited her up to his room. There he turned on the charm and seduced her. After she left, he ordered the biggest steak on the menu from room service, devoured it, and fell into a deep sleep.[6]

The next day was given over to interviews. Murphy charmed the reporters with his usual self-effacing humor and apparent lack of ego. The following morning, instead of flying to Dallas on American Airlines as had been planned, he hitched a ride with Associated Press reporter William Barnard and Lois Sager Foxhall, a writer for the *Dallas Morning News* and one of the nation's first female war correspondents. As the miles unfolded and the little towns passed by, Murphy began to relax. From sitting stiff and polite, he gradually sunk down into the back seat, looking out the window, watching the tranquil summertime countryside of central Texas roll past.

"This is what I came home to see," he said after a long silence. "You can't realize how swell this is until you have been away." They passed through San Marcos, Austin, Temple, and Waco. When the reporters asked him about his wartime experiences he said, "I just fought to stay alive like anybody else, I guess."[7]

As they drove towards Dallas, Murphy commented how different Texas was from what he had grown accustomed to in Europe. Here he did not have to worry about snipers on the bridges, "and all the houses were not half wrecked by bombs." During the long drive, he became less guarded and started opening up to the reporters. "Over there it was a helluva thing," he said. "I don't like to talk about it, but I'm telling you it was a helluva thing. It wasn't bad for me in Africa, but in Sicily and Italy and France it was bad."

And then there were buddies he left behind—they were never far from his thoughts. "Many a guy who wanted to come home worse than anything else in the world will stay over there forever. They are the fellows I want the honors to go to, not to me."

But despite what he might have wanted, he was bestrewn with honors. Most towns in and around Hunt County with any claim to Audie Murphy tried to out-do each other in welcome home parties for the returning hero. In little Celeste, where Murphy had first gone to school, there was a different spin—an attempt to emulate the humility of the town hero. "There will be no fanfare when Audie arrives," in Celeste, explained a Greenville newspaper, because the people there "realize that he is sincere in saying that he wants no heroes [sic] welcome."[8]

By contrast, the mayor of Farmersville, where Audie Murphy's sister still lived, said that Murphy was going to get the grandest reception any Farmersville boy ever got, "whether he likes it or not." It was the one chance they would have, he said, to put the little town on the map. None of Murphy's protestations to the contrary would deter the outbreak of civic boosterism. "When a boy from Farmersville [note that Murphy was now "from" Farmersville] wins medals all over Italy and then goes up to France and stands off a German army singlehanded and gets the Congressional Medal of Honor— he'll just have to count on making a few sacrifices when he gets back home."[9]

To be sure, Audie Murphy Day in Farmersville was a big, exciting event for the small town, probably the biggest in its history. The mayor travelled the twenty miles west to the town of McKinney where he met Murphy coming up from San Antonio. They rode together in a car on the way back, led by a McKinney fire engine, blaring its siren the entire way. They sped past dark green cotton fields to Farmersville, where workers were still building a stage on the town square for the festivities that would take place the next afternoon and which, among other things, would include a performance of patriotic tunes by the band of McKinney's Ashburn General Hospital, which had been an Army hospital since May 1943. Red, white, and blue bunting covered the square and the town was festooned with countless American and Texas flags.

Murphy's first stop, however, was his sister's house. The fire engine, siren still screaming, led him there. Cameras clicked as Murphy stepped out of the car, kissed his sister, shook hands with his brother-in-law, greeted a cousin, and patted the heads of his nephews. "How's everything?" he finally said, as though it were 1940 again and he had just hitchhiked over from Greenville for supper.

The bright June sun beat down, until the family retreated into the house, away from the cameras. Shortly after, his younger siblings arrived from the orphanage.

"Who told you you could wear lipstick?" he asked his sister Nadene. He had not seen her since she was eleven.

"He hasn't changed a bit," announced Corinne, "not a bit. I was afraid he would change, but he hasn't. All that has happened hasn't done a thing to him. I can see he's the same." More relatives arrived, and the group finally moved out to the downtown Coffee Shop Café, treating Murphy to a fried chicken dinner.[10]

The next day 5,000 people turned up to salute Audie Murphy— quite an achievement for a town of 2,200. They came from all over the county. "There was never so much honking and cheering and waving in Farmersville" as when Audie arrived at the downtown square, one reporter said.[11]

The ceremony started at 2:30 in the afternoon, by which time it was almost a hundred degrees. The front row of the crowd was mostly young boys, while far in the back a group of men in overalls stood up in the bed of a flatbed truck to see the stage. Many in the middle came in their Sunday best. Some had prudently brought umbrellas for shade.

Audie Murphy sat just to the left of the little lectern surrounded by the local dignitaries and was visibly uncomfortable with all the attention. The Ashburn Hospital band played its short concert to start the proceedings. Murphy kept his eyes mostly on his shoes as the speakers, like Colonel James B. Anderson, Commanding Officer of the Ashburn Hospital, praised his heroism. The mayor spoke. A banker spoke, and then presented Murphy with $1,750 worth of war bonds for which the locals had contributed. He shifted uneasily in his seat as the principal of the Farmersville Grammar School read an account of how he had held off the German attack at Holtzwihr and earned the Medal of Honor.

Finally after almost an hour and a half, it was his turn. Drops of sweat rolled down his baby-faced cheeks. He spoke quietly and it was not easy to hear him. Later he said that speaking to that first big audience "was worse than facing any machine gun." His natural shyness and humility precluded him from saying much.

"I know you people don't want to stand in this hot sun any longer and just look at me," Murphy said, but "I want to thank you one and all, and I'd like to say that you can be proud of your husbands and brothers and sweethearts who did the fighting over there. They did a swell job."

The crowd loved it and pressed around him as he stepped down off the stage. At one point, an old man in a blue cotton work shirt and blue denim trousers made his way through the throng to shake the hero's hand. "Thank you, boy, for all you did," he said. Murphy suddenly teared up. A nearby photographer raised his camera and shouted "Smile!" "Sometimes a fellow just can't," Murphy replied.[12]

For a few days, Audie Murphy stayed at his sister's house, but he came to realize that things were different now. Now he was the center of attention wherever he went. Everyone wanted to see him, everyone wanted to shake his hand, everyone wanted to know what he thought about this or that. On June 19 he went over to the Ashburn Hospital in McKinney to visit wounded soldiers. "I'd like to shake hands with every fellow in this place," he said, "and I'm coming back to do it, too." One reporter who was there noted that Murphy seemed more at ease with the soldiers than with civilians and that at the hospital Murphy had "really felt at home for the first time since he returned from the European battlefields." [13]

Innumerable photographers followed him from place to place hoping for the perfect picture. They were not above staging pictures either, which they did at the barber shop, at his sister's house, at neighbor's houses, at the café, everywhere. Many of these photos would have national circulation. He went to Dallas on June 20—his birthday—and visited an aunt. To his chagrin, even in the big city he was recognized. Several high school girls crowded around him for pictures and autographs. He was, after all, handsome and famous. For one of their autographs, he signed "Fugitive from the Law of Averages." Far more than being a hero, that was how he saw himself.

By sheer coincidence, actor Gary Cooper was in Dallas that day plugging his latest movie, a light-hearted western called *Along Came Jones*, at the grand Majestic Theater downtown. Murphy was excited to meet the man who was, once at least, his favorite actor. A photograph shows him in his full dress uniform, including his hat, beaming with a smile as he shakes Cooper's hand. Like so many other pictures of Murphy, it highlights just how young he could look, particularly compared with an older man in a dapper suit, a head taller than the famous combat veteran.

While in Dallas, Murphy spoke to business groups and visited the Dallas veterans' hospital where he returned to a familiar theme: "Those are the guys who ought to have these medals."

Back in Hunt County, Greenville determined to outdo Farmersville in its celebration of the local hero, and scheduled its own "Audie Murphy Day" for June 27. In the inevitable caravan of cars that arrived at Corinne's house to bring him to Greenville, Murphy rode in a highway patrol car rather than in the assigned limousine; and he and the patrolman, Everett Brandon, became lifelong friends. After lunch at the Rotary Club, yet another parade took Murphy to the Hunt County courthouse. The crowd was reported to exceed 10,000.

"That's what he wants," Murphy told the crowd in his brief remarks, speaking of all the soldiers who were now returning from the war. "He wants to come home and find home just as he left it." That certainly seemed to be Murphy's wish. He asked to be driven by the gas station and store where he had once worked.

Of course, one thing had changed dramatically—his celebrity. At one point, Murphy was besieged by a crowd of teenage girls seeking his autograph. He good-naturedly signed anything proffered, until Patrolman Everett Brandon pushed through the crowd and guided Murphy back to the car. "Lt. Audie Murphy Forced to Fall Back as Bobby Soxers Charge," quipped a headline.

A few days later he was back in Dallas. He made an appearance for Interstate Theaters and took part in a two-part performance on a Sunday afternoon Dallas radio show called "Showtime." One part was a simple interview. The other was a dramatic reenactment of the battle at Holtzwihr complete with the sound effects of battle and military music played by the theater's orchestra. James Cherry, an executive with Interstate, thought Murphy was a natural when it came to acting. If he was a natural, he was a natural in the manner of a Gary Cooper character: humble, shy, endearingly nervous, and genuine.

Murphy spent his first Fourth of July after coming home from Europe in McKinney where he gamely complied with an invitation to be the guest of honor at a three-day rodeo and horse show. Each night he led the horses and riders into the arena. A few days later he was inducted into the Veterans of Foreign Wars (VFW). Later in the summer he endured another "Audie Murphy Day," this one in Corsicana, Texas, a small town southeast of Dallas in Navarro County that made absolutely no claim to having any connection to him at all.

Murphy was good-natured, polite, and though he did not like public speaking, he also did not like to turn people down, which meant he was kept distractingly busy with events. In between, he went back to Celeste to see the Cawthon's and went hunting with Mr. Cawthon again. He visited with Haney Lee and saw some other old friends. Early in July he requested extended leave, deferring his return to the Army until the middle of August at which point he would begin the formal process for his discharge from the service.

In August, he bought an old two-story house with a big front porch in Farmersville. He paid $850 for the farmhouse and another $750 for all the furniture in it, using money from war bonds that the citizenry had given him. The house was big enough so that his three youngest siblings could move out of the orphan's home and live there with Corinne and her family.

Early one morning, Corinne went to Murphy's bedroom to wake him so he could go hunting. She found him sitting up with the light on. "I didn't sleep a minute last night," he told her. "I fought the damned war all night long." Another night she awoke to discover her brother had turned on all the lights in the house. He quietly told her that the lights helped keep him awake. Sleep, he said, only brought on nightmares. When he visited his aunt and her daughter in Dallas he woke them up yelling for the men in his company. Other friends he visited found him jittery. Unexpected sounds caused him to jump. A plate of black-eyed peas at lunch caused him to freeze and then leave the table. Only later did he admit that they had reminded him of the brains of a German soldier he had seen shot in the head. Monroe Hackney, a good friend with whom Murphy had spent a lot of time before the war going back to his days in Celeste, simply said that his friend seemed "mixed up" that summer.

Audie Murphy was also thinking about what he would do with his life after the adulation died away, once his anonymity returned. He considered everything from continuing in the Army to working as a radio repairman to becoming a veterinarian. He had a few reasonably solid job offers. Jake Bowen offered to take him back on at the radio repair shop. Interstate Theaters executive James Cherry offered him a job as a theater manager. Everett Brandon offered to help him get an interview with the Texas Highway Patrol. The chairman of the *Dallas Morning News* offered personally to pay his way through any college he wanted to attend. Another executive at the paper offered to make him a reporter.

But Murphy's postwar career came from the most unexpected source imaginable, and it all began with his picture.

CHAPTER EIGHT

# A HERO GOES TO HOLLYWOOD

I n the 1940s, *Life* magazine was an American arbiter of all the people, ideas, and trends worth knowing about. Most of its content came in the form of photo essays, which could have a powerful emotional impact. Very often its weekly cover photo became an icon. In the summer of 1945 it featured people who were becoming cultural touchstones: people like British Prime Minister Winston Churchill, American General Douglas MacArthur, and popular Hollywood actor Jimmy Stewart wearing his U.S. Army Air Corps uniform. The July 21 issue featured a youthful and beaming Audie L. Murphy on the cover with the caption "Most Decorated Soldier." His popularity, about which he already felt ambivalent, exploded. Readers of *Life* had seen plenty of pictures about the harsh reality of war. They knew what a combat infantryman's face looked like—haggard, unshaven, unwashed. But Murphy was the perfect embodiment of what Americans *wanted* their returning soldiers to look like: youthful, innocent, healthy and "all-American." Murphy's face fit with how *Life* readers thought about America. It could have been the face of an eager boy going to the senior prom, or of the high school quarterback who had won the state championship, or the young lifeguard at the local pool, or, as it turned out, of America's greatest soldier, a face that reassuringly had no scars and no hint of the horrors its eyes had witnessed. His was the face mothers hoped to see when they finally got their sons back from the war, the living embodiment of Norman Rockwell's famous painting *Homecoming G.I.* which had appeared on the cover of the *Saturday Evening Post* that May.

In a photo essay inside the magazine entitled "*Life* Visits Audie Murphy," wholesome image piled upon wholesome image. Here was Audie at the local barbershop getting his first haircut after returning home, while just outside the window a stiffly-posed crowd of men watched. There was Audie sipping a Coca-Cola with a family friend. Here was Audie petting a dog, or chatting with a farmer at the city limits sign, or showing his younger sister the German sniper's rifle he brought home. There was Murphy and his sister's family gathered around the table for supper. And finally, here is the all-American boy with his "special girl," whom *Life* identified as Mary Lee, looking deeply into each other's eyes as she straightens his uniform tie. "Audie hopes she is his own girl," explains the caption, "but he isn't quite sure yet because he usually blushes when he gets within ten feet of any girl."

Mary Lee was a complete fabrication by the magazine to fit the image it was trying to construct, but this was how most Americans got their first look at the most decorated soldier in the history of the U.S. Army. His appearance on *Life*'s cover took him from being a celebrity in places like Corsicana, McKinney, and Greenville, to being one of the most recognizable faces in the entire country overnight. It also brought him to the attention of actor James Cagney.

Cagney was among the most popular and highly regarded stars in Hollywood. In the 1930s he had played several tough guy and gangster roles and was one of Warner Brothers' most bankable stars. In 1939 he signed a new three-year, eleven-movie contract that would pay him $150,000 per picture, plus 10 percent of any movie profits over $1 million. In 1942 he won an Academy Award for his portrayal of American Broadway composer and entertainer George M. Cohan in *Yankee Doodle Dandy*.

In 1942, Cagney and his brother Bill formed Cagney Productions and agreed to produce five movies for United Artists to distribute over five years. The company finished its first production, *Johnny Come Lately*, starring Cagney himself, in 1943. The reviews stung. The *New York Times* called it "palpably amateurish in production and direction." Most others critics tended to agree. "It made money," Cagney said later, "but it was no winner." By then his company was in negotiations to buy the film rights to the Broadway hit *Oklahoma!* but the deal fell through, another blow to the company's image. When Cagney's second film, *Blood on the Sun*, came out in 1945, it did even worse at the box office than the company's previous effort. Cagney Productions desperately needed a shot of new energy.[1]

Cagney had been a prominent Hollywood supporter of the war effort. He had gone overseas on a USO tour in 1944, been deeply involved in war bond drives, and made movies for the War Department. When Cagney saw Audie Murphy on the cover of *Life* magazine, he was captivated, as many Americans were, but he also regarded Murphy with the eye of a professional moviemaker. From the evidence of the magazine, Cagney thought the young hero photographed well from every angle; the Cagney company could use a fresh face, fresh talent, and if it happened to come from a war hero so much the better.

One afternoon a telegram arrived at Corinne's house addressed to Audie Murphy. They could hardly believe it when they saw it was from James Cagney inviting Murphy to come out to Hollywood to meet him, get a look at the movie business, and be his guest for a while. Cagney was one of Murphy's favorite actors, but he was so overwhelmed by the offer that he dithered over whether to accept it. He asked everyone he knew what they thought of it and what he should do. Then a second telegram arrived, repeating the offer. Murphy finally agreed.

He soon had second thoughts. He told a Corsicana reporter that he was dreading flying to California. In part this was because he was under the misapprehension that Cagney wanted to do a movie about his life. Murphy did not want to be under any greater spotlight than he already was. Nevertheless, on the morning of September 20, 1945, Murphy boarded an American Airlines flight from Dallas to Los Angeles. He wore his Army uniform (it was one day before his official discharge from the Army as a first lieutenant on fifty percent disability) and had all of eleven dollars in his pocket.

Waiting for him when he landed was none other than Jimmy Cagney himself, one of the most recognizable men in Hollywood. Audie Murphy, however, looked nothing like the photos from his *Life* magazine shot. "When I met him at the plane, I got the shock of my life," Cagney said later. Murphy seemed nervous and looked completely exhausted, so different from the beaming face he had seen on the cover of *Life* that Cagney decided to take him to his guesthouse and have him stay there instead of in a hotel. "I was afraid he might jump out a window" without any supervision, Cagney said. Cagney's own house was comfortable and grand and opulent like no private residence Murphy had ever seen. If this was the sort of money that could be made in the movie business, then perhaps he should give it serious thought.[2]

The idea of bringing Audie Murphy out to Hollywood "was impulsiveness on my part," Cagney told a movie columnist. Cagney sensed a "spiritual overtone" in Murphy's "assurance and poise without aggressiveness."[3]

Cagney and Murphy got to know each other reasonably well. When they were in public together, Murphy was embarrassed by the attention he received, and visibly winced whenever he was called a hero. Cagney found Murphy's humility and self-effacement very appealing.

For a couple of weeks, Audie Murphy observed Hollywood while Hollywood observed Audie Murphy. "When Audie was seen here and there in Cagney's company," explained a reporter for the *Houston Chronicle*, "offers began to pour in from movie producers." He also met people who urged him to write a book about his wartime experiences. He turned down every offer seeing them as "mostly publicity gimmicks." He was determined not to trade on his war record or medals; whatever attention fell on him should be deflected, he felt, to the men of his company and to the men who had died in combat. Still, Murphy enjoyed meeting movie stars like Spencer Tracy and Robert Montgomery, and when Cagney bade Murphy goodbye, the star actor was convinced that the wartime hero had Hollywood potential.[4]

---

Home in Texas, Murphy traveled to San Antonio, where Carolyn Price was now a nurse at Brook Army Medical Center at Fort Sam

Houston. She was taken aback by the sight of Audie Murphy in civilian clothes. The only time she had ever seen him out of uniform was wearing a hospital gown in Aix-en-Provence. She had seen the cover of *Life*, and knew the sort of reception he had been given when he got home. Much to her delight, she quickly discovered that he had not changed. "I could detect no vanity, no sign of overbearing arrogance," she said. She told Murphy that she worried about him going into the movie business. Its fickleness and artificiality seemed a bad match for his virtues. He smiled his tired smile. He understood her worry, but there was a simple reason he was choosing that course. He needed the money.

Soon Cagney called and offered him a contract and this time Murphy did not hesitate. By the end of the year—a year that began with him as a convalescing soldier in an army hospital in Europe and ended with his being one of the most famous names in the United States—Audie Murphy had left Texas, along with his interests in being a soldier, a mercenary, a veterinarian, or a radio repairman, and moved to Hollywood.

"I thought it would be kind of nice to keep him like family, so we put him up in a house I owned next door to us," Cagney explained when Murphy arrived to begin his new life. Cagney paid Murphy a weekly stipend of $150. But Murphy's first job was simply to fish, ride horses, and do whatever he needed to do to rest and regain his health.

Once he felt settled, Murphy began taking acting classes. Cagney enrolled him at the Actors Laboratory, a noted drama school in Hollywood. He registered as "Bill Murphy" in hopes of anonymity. "I am fine and working every day," Murphy wrote in March 1946. "The work is easy, it consists mostly of reading and learning to speak lines correctly."

It might have been easy compared to picking cotton, but it was a demanding course. The curriculum at the Actors Lab involved twenty-seven hours of acting lessons per week, supplemented by three hours of lectures on topics like script reading and film history, two hours of speech and diction, and an hour each of fencing and body movement work. It's not many students who have thirty-four hours of coursework a week. Murphy needed it all. He had an ambling walk that Cagney derisively referred to as a "hayshaker," and his thick Texas accent was all but unintelligible to some of his fellow students. "It is not standard speech for stage and screen," one of his teachers remarked.[5]

More troubling to Murphy than the academic demands were the radical politics of the faculty. He thought they insinuated politics into everything with the goal of indoctrinating newcomers into communism. "There were a lot of leftists and Commie lovers in it," he said frankly. "I was an ignorant country boy but even I could see that they were teaching communism and not acting." Murphy's reaction was not without foundation. Actors Lab teachers were notorious for having communist sympathies. The *Hollywood Reporter* said that its founders were as "red as a burlesque queen's garters." Murphy found the strident politics of the Actors Lab extremely irritating, and finally quit the school at the end of the summer.[6]

But even though Murphy hated communist proselytizing, he also signed his name to a petition emblazoned "Hollywood Fights Back," circulated by actors, directors and producers who were "disgusted and outraged by the continuing attempt of the House Committee on Un-American Activities to smear the Motion Picture Industry" as a hotbed of communism.[7]

In Hollywood, communism divided the left. There were indeed Communist Party members or communist sympathizers. There were also liberals who thought communism was no particular threat and those who were liberal Cold Warriors, many of whom, like Ronald Reagan, ended up on the right. As one of Ronald Reagan's biographers has noted, Reagan, then a Democrat and head of the Screen

Actors Guild, "discovered himself in the middle of a struggle between liberal and communist elements for control" of various Hollywood organizations, especially trade unions. Reagan "had known communists before, but he had never been exposed to their tenacious organizational combativeness."[8]

In April 1946, Murphy spoke at a meeting of the Beverly Hills chapter of the American Veterans Committee. Murphy, like many others, including Ronald Reagan who served on its Hollywood membership board, assumed that the AVC was simply a pro-veterans group, which among other issues focused on finding affordable housing for veterans, but in fact it was, as one historian has written, "one of the most left-leaning of a variety of groups appealing to returning servicemen." It was intended, by its leadership, to be a liberal answer to groups like the conservative American Legion. The next year, to draw attention to the troubles that returning veterans were having finding affordable housing, Murphy, along with actors Van Heflin, Melvyn Douglas, and Eddie Albert, starred in a play called *The Case of the Missing Homes.*[9]

The AVC speech was one of Murphy's first public appearances in Hollywood and in attendance were big names like Douglas Fairbanks Jr., Tyrone Power, and Robert Montgomery (all of whom were veterans: Power in the Marine Corps, Fairbanks and Montgomery in the Navy). That night Murphy also met Will Rogers Jr., the son of the famous humorist and an aspiring Democrat politician. Later that year Rogers ran for the U.S. Senate with the support of Audie Murphy, Reagan, Orson Welles, and numerous others. In November 1947, Murphy spoke briefly at a rally against HUAC and its methods, saying what it was doing was "a challenge to the liberties for which our servicemen fought." These were strong words coming from the most decorated soldier of the war. The FBI took note of his conspicuous presence at the rally and started a file on him.[10]

Seeing in Murphy a potentially appealing candidate for the left, if indeed that's where his sentiments lay, Dore Schary, a political liberal and high-ranking executive at Metro-Goldwyn-Mayer, invited Audie Murphy to his house for a visit. There he tried to get him to run for Congress in the fall of 1948. "I can't even make a living," Murphy responded. "Why would I want to run for Congress?" Murphy left after only a few minutes, once he realized that was all Schary wanted him for.[11]

Murphy was a man of neither the ideological left nor the right, but a patriot. In 1948, for example, he spoke out against communist infiltration of veterans' organizations. That year he also endorsed Douglas MacArthur for president. If he merited any political label, it was probably conservative Southern Democrat.

———————

Much as he hated the Actors Lab, he met an actress there with whom he began a passionate affair. Her name was Jean Peters and she was a beauty queen from Ohio. Like Murphy, she was trying to break into the movie business; she was under contract to 20th Century Fox. They were very close for a summer, but Peters abandoned Murphy once she caught the eye of eccentric millionaire Howard Hughes. Murphy steamed about it for months, threatening to fight Hughes if ever he saw him, and condemning the greed and naked ambition he thought drove Peters to toss him aside.

Murphy was handsome and youthful-looking on the outside, but on the inside he was a bundle of frayed nerves and jagged emotions. Because Murphy did not like being alone, Cagney assigned his old friend and publicity agent Charles Leonard to live with him. Murphy, however, was not an easy housemate. Even with the prescription sleeping pills that he took, Murphy suffered severe nightmares and would often wake in the middle of the night screaming. Leonard, rather high-strung himself, would then leap from his bed and charge through the house with a gun. On one occasion, Murphy woke just in time to keep Leonard from shooting him. Nightmares apart, there were no hard feelings between the two men and Leonard in fact introduced Audie Murphy to the woman who became his first wife. Murphy saw a picture of a pretty, dark-haired young actress named Wanda Hendrix on the cover of the February 1946 issue of *Coronet* magazine and he was smitten. The diminutive Hendrix (she was 5'2") was from Jacksonville, Florida, and had come to Hollywood fiercely determined to build a movie career. She landed her first role in a feature film in Warner Brothers' 1945 *Confidential Agent* starring Charles Boyer, Lauren Bacall, and Peter Lorre. At Murphy's urging, Leonard prevailed upon Cagney to host a dinner party and invite Hendrix. Cagney did as he was bidden, and while Murphy was transfixed, Hendrix did not take to him right away, repeatedly turning him down for dates.

Still, "if it hadn't been for Wanda," Murphy said later, "I would never have stayed in this town." He determined to stay because he wanted to make enough money so that she would consider him a serious suitor and potential husband.[12]

By the summer of 1946, Murphy was appearing regularly in the pages of *Variety* and other trade papers, which reported his public appearances (like his September trip to Staten Island's Halloran Army Hospital, the largest hospital of its type in the world) and rumors of films in which Cagney might cast him. One report said that Cagney Productions was grooming him "for important roles in 'The Stray Lamb' and 'A Lion Is in the Streets,' both to star James Cagney." In September, *Variety* reported he would play the starring role in *Two Soldiers*, "probably because he was one soldier who won enough medals for two." Like so many Hollywood rumors, these rumors eventually proved false.[13]

Hollywood also read about an adventure Murphy had in December 1946 on a visit home to Texas. Murphy had picked up a hitchhiker near the little town of Vickery. He was a big man wearing what looked like an army jacket, and after getting in the front seat, he jammed a jacketed hand into Murphy's side, saying he had a gun. Murphy twice told him to pull his hand away, and when he did not, Murphy stopped the car and pummeled him. He then drove to a nearby gas station and called his highway patrol friend Everett Brandon.

There is a photo of Murphy explaining the story to two highway patrol officers and a third man, possibly from the Dallas County sheriff's office, as they stand alongside his car. The passenger door is open and Murphy's tie is undone. It looks like a staged photo. The story was picked up in the papers and in cynical Hollywood was suspected of being a publicity stunt, which vexed Murphy very much.[14]

———————

Given the limited progress made by Cagney Productions, and in Murphy's acting ability, Cagney was willing to loan his trainee actor to another studio. Wanda Hendrix's agent then landed him a small part in the Paramount film *Beyond Glory*. The film starred Alan Ladd as a World War II hero and winner of the Distinguished Service Cross who after the war enrolls at West Point as a cadet. Murphy was cast as Ladd's West Point roommate. Location shooting began at the Military Academy in the first week of September.

Murphy turned in a workman-like job in his three scenes. He had minimal dialogue, and the high point of his performance was a scene where he cut in and danced with Donna Reed. He looked dashing, however, in a West Point cadet uniform.

"Audie has as much natural acting talent as any newcomer I've ever worked with," said John Farrow, the film's director. As always, Murphy was charmingly self-deprecating about his lack of experience. "I had eight words to say," he said, "seven more than I could handle."[15]

Murphy received $3,000 for his work on the movie. Under the terms of his contract, Cagney Productions should have received half of the money, but they declined and let him have the full payment. Another windfall from the movie was his meeting a man named David McClure who would become one of Audie Murphy's closest friends and working partners.

McClure, fourteen years older than Murphy, was Phi Beta Kappa member from the University of North Carolina, and came across to the weary young Texan as something of a bookish sort. He called him "Spec," because he wore spectacles. They got on well together in part because McClure was a combat veteran as well, having served in the Signal Corps in Europe. After his discharge from the Army, McClure became a staff writer at Universal-International, wrote for movie magazines, and served for a time as Walt Disney's personal writer. He was also an assistant to famed gossip columnist Hedda Hopper.

Hopper was the premier gossip columnist and rumor spreader in Hollywood in the 1940s and 1950s. "She told motion picture executives, housewives and teenagers which film star was pregnant, who was about to elope and who might become the newest star." Because McClure had her ear, it was in this last capacity that Hopper became one of Audie Murphy's greatest champions. She was "a judge and censor of all that went on in Hollywood." She had a political side as well, and was a determined Cold Warrior who corresponded with FBI head J. Edgar Hoover so often that they were on a first name basis. She encouraged him in his suspicions of communist actions in Hollywood.[16]

*Beyond Glory* marked the end of Audie Murphy's association with Jimmy Cagney. Remarkably perhaps, given Hollywood's reputation for brittle personalities and bitter breakups, there were no hard feelings. "It turned out we had no use for him really," Cagney reflected later with candor. "He couldn't act." With the dissolution of his relationship with Cagney Productions, Audie Murphy moved out of Cagney's guesthouse.[17]

Murphy's prospects seemed bleak. He wound up sleeping in the back room of a gym owned by a friend, Terry Hunt, an Army veteran who had served in Southeast Asia during the war. In the gym, one of his star customers was Clark Gable, himself a vet. But in the back room, Hunt opened his doors to any returning vets who were down on their luck. There were a lot of these in Hollywood in 1947, many drifting around looking for work in the movies. At one point, Hunt had eight otherwise homeless veterans living at his gym. Murphy slept on a cot, worked out in the gym, and scraped by on his army pension of $87 a month. He was so broke, he joked to a friend, that his usual diet was "a shower for breakfast and a steam bath for lunch." Eventually he moved into a small house owned by Hunt.[18]

While waiting for his big break, he continued to make public appearances. In October 1947, for instance, he was in Dallas along with five other Medal of Honor winners for a gala luncheon with Admiral Chester Nimitz.[19]

And, because it was a seemingly necessary part of trying to break into acting, he still made the rounds of Hollywood parties even though he disliked them intensely. He did not drink, disliked dancing, and abhorred the typical phony small-talk that went on at them. "I hate to waste an evening prattling nonsense," he said. But at least he usually had Wanda Hendrix with him. He and Wanda were now "going steady," the newspapers dutifully reported. In the middle of November 1947, *Life* magazine ran a photo essay on Audie and

Wanda that emphasized their storybook courtship. "Starlet Wanda Hendrix goes steady with war's most decorated soldier," said the headline. Photos showed Murphy showing his medals to a smiling Hendrix, who looks up at him fondly. "At present," said the caption, "Audie and Wanda consider each other more important than any career. They are reportedly engaged and the love affair, unlike so many in moviedom, is said to be the real thing." There was even a photo of Murphy having tea with Hendrix and her mother, who in actuality was intensely skeptical of their relationship. "I don't think it's very serious," she said a little later. A mother's disapproval would not deter *Life*, however. "At tea time Audie calls frequently at the Hendrix home," and Mrs. Hendrix "thoroughly approves of him." The two appeared together in a saccharine ad for the Lane Furniture Company and its cedar hope chest, the perfect gift for happy couples who were about to tie the knot.[20]

One Hollywood party in particular added to Audie Murphy's image of being a tough guy behind his baby face and humble demeanor. Lawrence Tierney, a B-movie actor known as much for his drinking and numerous arrests as his movie roles, was irritating Murphy by his behavior, particularly his constant butting into the conversation he was having with Wanda. Twice Murphy coolly asked him to tone down his language in front of his date. Twice Tierney brushed him off. The third time Murphy approached him there was something different in his eyes and he ordered the man to leave. Tierney left. "If somebody hadn't stopped me," Murphy said later, "I would have happily killed him." The scene was notable enough that *Variety* reported it. "Such deadly menace I never saw in anybody's eyes," said a reporter who watched the scene play out.[21]

David McClure, who was convinced of Murphy's talents, helped him land his next role, a bit part in a forgettable comedy entitled *Texas, Brooklyn and Heaven* in which he played a newspaper boy for a Dallas newspaper. For his few minutes on screen he received $500. While Murphy appreciated the opportunity the small part offered him, he resolved that from now on, he would take leading parts or nothing, and declined several other small parts in various movies.

He also decided that he would write his wartime memoirs after all, to honor the men with whom he served. He already had 350 pages of notes that he had written in a school composition book, jotting down memories whenever the spirit moved him to pick up his pen. McClure thought so much of Murphy's project that he dropped his other jobs to help Murphy write the book, in exchange for 40 percent of whatever Murphy earned from it. By March 1948 they had completed five chapters. *Variety* jokingly referred to the ongoing project as his "Audiebiography."[22]

Murphy now had his own little apartment, and it was there that he and McClure would meet to write the book. Murphy provided his notes, sometimes wrote passages himself (he wrote in first person and often showed a good, dramatic narrative sense), and at other times would simply lie back and stare at the ceiling and let the vivid stories tumble out of his memory while McClure wrote them down. Murphy initially wanted to call the book *For a Young Man's Heart*—not exactly what the public expected for a wartime memoir. They eventually came up with the much better, instantly memorable title *To Hell and Back.*[23]

An early draft of the book began, "Often yet, when asleep in the heart of a great American city, I dream of battle; and the furious sounds of combat gather about my bed." Murphy's first edit was minor. "I awake in a cold sweat of fear and alertness ~~with a cry on my lips: 'Get down! Get down!'~~ Then gradually I become aware of the hum of the city about me; see its vast reflection of lights through my windows; and know that all is well. Peace has come. The engines of war are still."[24]

"I switch on a light, reach for a sedative; and the long procession of phantom dead begins again in the brain," the manuscript continued. McClure later noted on the draft pages "I believe that Audie Murphy objected to the first two pages as being too emotional. Also he was having nightmares at the time and did not want the public to know." Nor did Murphy want the public to know that he relied on sleeping pills. Eventually they decided to begin the book with Murphy's initiation into combat during the invasion of Sicily.

While Murphy and McClure were working on the manuscript, an invitation arrived from the French government asking if the celebrated Lieutenant Murphy would come to Paris as the official guest of the president for the presentation to him of the Legion of Honor and a second Croix de Guerre. He accepted the invitation in large part to go back to the battlefields on which he had fought.

He took part in Bastille Day celebrations in Paris, received his awards at Les Invalides, the French soldiers' memorial and the site of Napoleon's tomb, and then hopped a train south to the Riviera. Murphy and McClure started on Yellow Beach and retraced the path of Company B. They hiked up "Pill Box Hill" and Murphy unerringly found the exact spot at which Tipton had been killed. Up the Rhone Valley the men travelled, Murphy offering clear memories in a subdued voice, which went silent if anyone other than the two of them were present, McClure continually jotting down notes. In the forest outside of Holtzwihr, they discovered the very tank destroyer upon which Murphy had won the Medal of Honor. It was covered with brush but outside of being weathered, it was largely unchanged. Murphy was shocked to see how little the countryside and the towns had been cleaned up since the war. In several of those towns he received a warm welcome from grateful residents.

On their way back to Los Angeles, the men stopped in New York to sign a contract for the book with the Henry Holt Company.

Murphy was given a $1,500 advance. Holt wanted the manuscript finished by October. It was a tight deadline, especially given the number of public appearances Murphy had already agreed to do, including one for the opening of a rodeo arena named after him in north Texas.

In mid-October 1948, Murphy started work on the first movie in which he would play the lead role. Allied Artists' *Bad Boy* was a juvenile delinquent film in which Murphy played a young thief named Danny Lester sent to a boys' ranch in central Texas for rehabilitation. His costars Jane Wyatt and Lloyd Nolan helped with tips and coaching, which, he said, "bolstered my confidence considerably." Wyatt admitted that the other actors regarded Murphy as "a curiosity. He was the cutest little boy and so very nice, but he was by no means a forceful figure on the set." Others remembered that he was constantly battling stomach trouble during the shoot, and was always slipping away to vomit. He had recently been diagnosed with an ulcer, the treatment of which required him to adhere to a strict diet.[25]

*Bad Boy* received mixed reviews, as did Murphy's performance. One critic called the movie "hackneyed, insipid, and illogical," and asked why Audie Murphy was even in the film. The reason for his presence was "neither apparent nor reasonable in other than exploitation terms, for he is obviously not a criminal and he is not over-able to act." Regardless of its reception, the project held a special place in Audie Murphy's life for a couple of reasons. The movie was funded by Variety Clubs International, which ran a Boys Ranch in Copperas Cove, Texas, where his youngest brother was now living after leaving the Boles Orphans Home. As a measure of how he felt about the organization, in September before filming began, and with the due date for the *To Hell and Back* manuscript looming, Murphy went to Washington, D.C., for an appearance at the Variety Clubs' Humanitarian Award dinner. He wore his full dress uniform with all his decorations and stole the show.[26]

The movie also changed the trajectory of his career. After it came out, executives at Universal-International, one of the major studios of the day, offered him a seven-year contract for $100,000 a year, seeing real promise in the young war hero turned actor. Murphy accepted Universal's offer. It looked like he might actually have a shot in Hollywood, after all, and the publication of his memoirs changed his life even more.

CHAPTER NINE

# THE MAKING OF A STAR

E arly in 1949, Audie Murphy was starting to rebound from the doldrums in which his fledgling career had languished only a short time before. With much fanfare from the press, if not in the modest ceremony itself, he and Wanda Hendrix were finally married early in January, and honeymooned in and around Dallas.

In May, filming began for the second movie in which Murphy would be the star. *The Kid from Texas* was the first film under his new contract with Universal-International and was a fresh, as well as historically inaccurate, retelling of the story of Billy the Kid with Murphy in the title role. "As a youngster, I read everything about Billy I could get my hands on," he said. He wanted to play Billy "as a quiet guy, a real human being who made mistakes at times, instead of a swaggering superman." Murphy showed off his skill with pistols (shooting squirrels out of trees to entertain the crew), but was rather

109

less successful at portraying emotion. But if his acting was on the wooden side, he performed well enough. He was still finding his way as an actor, though he had already found the genre that suited him best—westerns.[1]

More importantly, however, that year saw the publication of *To Hell and Back* in February. Unlike his acting, his book won nearly universal praise. On March 10, it appeared on the *New York Times* bestseller list where it remained until the middle of June, peaking at number eight. He characteristically hoped that it would "remind a forgetful public of a lot of boys who never made it home." Two of those boys had their name on the dedication page: Lattie Tipton and Joe Sieja.

Murphy's pre-war life story is told in brief flashbacks and, purposefully, these do not add up to an autobiography. The book was meant as a memorial to his buddies and a testament to the price of their valor. "You would never know from his book that he is the most decorated soldier of the war," Charles Poore wrote in the *New York Times*, because *To Hell and Back* focuses little on the events for which Murphy won fame and medals.[2]

In early March 1949 as part of the ongoing publicity for *To Hell and Back*, Murphy appeared on NBC's weekly radio program *This Is Your Life*. His childhood friend Monroe Hackney was on the show, as was one of his first teachers from Celeste. Walter Weispfennig, who in 1945 was Murphy's forward artillery spotter in the battle at Holtzwihr and filed one of the eyewitness accounts that led to his Medal of Honor, was there as well. The most surprising guest on the show was Claudine Tipton, the daughter of his war buddy Lattie. Her appearance left him nearly speechless with emotion. He later presented her with the Distinguished Service Cross he won on the day her father was killed in action.[3]

By the next year, Murphy claimed he had given all his medals away. "I've been fed up with that 'most decorated' business for a long time," he said. "I realize that it is an honor, but only because it symbolizes the work done by a lot of other guys too." Supposedly, he had given most of his medals—including his Medal of Honor—to kids, but he couldn't precisely remember. In fact, he had not given all his medals away, but his assertion that he had was a testament to how uncomfortable he was with the adulation of his war record. "He feels deeply the loss of his comrades who didn't come back from the war," noted the Hollywood reporter who wrote the story.[4]

In late summer 1949, Murphy went to Utah to shoot his second western, *Sierra*, which costarred Wanda Hendrix, the only movie the two made together. Whenever there was a break in the filming, Murphy threw dice with the cast and crew. "He was a natural at the game," remembered costar James Arness, "and seemed to win everything." At night, he could be found at The Black Cat, a popular drinking and gambling spot tucked in behind the picturesque Parry Lodge motel. When Murphy learned that Dee Crosby, an Army veteran who had been in the hospital in Italy with him, lived nearby, he often invited him and his family to dinner at the Lodge.[5]

While the studio took every opportunity to play up the fact that Murphy and his wife were starring in a movie together, it was widely rumored that the two were not getting along. Early in the filming, Murphy commented that in his first eight months of marriage he had been "fighting harder than on eight European fronts." In a remark that gave readers a glimpse into the home life of the couple, *Variety* said "this is a spirited pair and if they scream at each other so let 'em scream."[6]

By the end of filming, Murphy announced that he and Hendrix were separating, scuttling studio plans to use their storybook marriage to sell the movie. Both avowed that they wanted to make the marriage work, to avoid a divorce, but Murphy acknowledged that divorce was likely. "Audie is not well," Hendrix said. "He's all mixed up." As he went back to Texas to get away from Hollywood for a while, Murphy conceded that Hendrix had done her best; the trouble was with him. "She had no more right around me than a lamb around a grizzly," he said.[7]

Hollywood was split on who was more to blame for the break-up. One studio executive made the not very patriotic statement that returning veterans often did not make the best husbands. But a veteran Hollywood writer countered, "the truth is that actresses, not war veterans, are the most difficult human beings to live with." In truth, it had never been a strong marriage. Hendrix was a sociable, ambitious actress and wanted to be seen at the right Hollywood parties. Murphy was a quiet, brooding, highly strung character, who had never liked the Tinseltown social life, and now that he was starring in westerns was even more inclined to dismiss it.[8]

Audie Murphy also liked guns, while Hendrix came to fear them, most especially in his hands. His gun collection was "the big thing in his life" and he cleaned them every day and, as she later said, "caressed them for hours." He slept with a loaded gun under his pillow and alarmed her with his screaming nightmares about combat. When they had arguments, she said, he sometimes pulled out a gun and aimed it at her, before turning it around and putting it in his mouth. He fired guns in the house, shooting clocks off the wall, shooting mirrors, shooting light switches. Once during their separation he shot the lock off the door of their apartment just to show her he could get in any time he wanted.[9]

In February 1950, she filed for divorce, citing mental cruelty as the reason. "Mr. Murphy's war record is well known," said the judge as he gaveled the marriage to an end, "and I am sure it contributed a great deal to his attitude."[10]

"He had the most beautiful smile," Wanda Hendrix said years later, "but unfortunately he never smiled much." Audie Murphy was, she said, "an ancient young man." Murphy's friend David McClure was blunter in his assessment. "It is generally assumed that Audie easily re-adjusted to civilian life, making a fortune as a movie star and living relatively happily ever after. Almost the reverse is true. Let us hope that God did forgive him. His battered nervous system never did."[11]

---

Early in 1950, the big news in Hollywood was that director John Huston was going to make a movie of Stephen Crane's classic Civil War novel *The Red Badge of Courage*. Huston wrote the screenplay himself and the town was abuzz with whom he might cast in the project. There were rumors, however, that the film was causing division in the upper ranks of MGM, with Dore Schary, the studio's head of production, enthusiastic about the project, and Louis B. Mayer, the founder and president of the studio, dead-set against it. The internal studio drama was so great that the *New Yorker* dispatched a reporter to follow the story.

Huston was known for directing Humphrey Bogart in celebrated films like *The Maltese Falcon, The Treasure of the Sierra Madre*, and *Key Largo*. He had just finished *The Asphalt Jungle*, for which he had also written the screenplay. While he had set up his own production company, he was under contract to direct one movie per year for MGM. He wanted to film Crane's novel not as a typical war movie full of action sequences, but as a psychological study of how battle affected the men who fought it, and, to that point, he wanted to avoid casting traditional Hollywood action stars.

When word leaked that Huston was writing the screenplay, hundreds of actors campaigned for roles in the film. Hedda Hopper used her column to push Audie Murphy for the starring role in the movie, even invoking geopolitics as a reason for Murphy to be cast. "With so many of our young men going to Korea," she said, "putting Audie in the picture would aid in boosting their morale."[12]

Though Murphy read for a part in the film, without Huston present, he had never made a movie with such a famous director and assumed he would not be chosen. Indeed, after doing publicity junkets for *The Kid from Texas*, which premiered in Dallas in March, and then for *Sierra*, which opened in Seattle in May, he asked Universal-International to cast him in a comedy.

Universal, however, saw him as a western star. Murphy made *Kansas Raiders* for U-I in May and June 1949. In it he played a young Jesse James, who was just beginning his days with Quantrill's Raiders. If he was still stiff in delivering lines and expressing emotion, he made a believable action star. In one scene, where Murphy shoots a man, his costar James Best recalled Murphy's eyes changing in an unsettling way. "I suddenly saw the man who went through World War II and had killed a lot of guys," Best said. "His looks chilled me."[13]

Huston finally met Murphy and something in the taciturn veteran won him over. Others involved with the movie were intensely skeptical of him both in terms of his unpredictable personality and his evident limitations as an actor. Schary, who had signed on as executive producer, and Gottfried Reinhardt, the film's producer, tried to talk Huston out of casting Murphy. "They'd rather have a star," Huston acknowledged. "They just don't see Audie the way I do."[14]

By August, Huston had cast most of the parts, including the surprise choice of World War II veteran and "Willie and Joe" cartoonist Bill Mauldin in the role of the "Loud Soldier." (Stephen Crane identified most of his characters by their descriptions and downplayed their names, underscoring the universality of the effects of war on the men who fight it.) "I think it's a damn fool idea," Mauldin said of his being cast. "But I'll go along with it." The choice for the lead—the "Young

Audie Murphy in his field uniform during basic training at Camp Wolters, Texas, summer 1942.
*Source: Audie Murphy/American Cotton Museum*

After a hunting trip with John Cawthon, probably summer 1945.
*Source: Audie Murphy/American Cotton Museum*

General Alexander Patch of the U.S. Seventh Army pins the Legion of Merit decoration on Audie Murphy during the ceremony in which he also received the Medal of Honor (the ribbon of which is visible around his neck), June 2, 1945.
*Source: Audie Murphy/American Cotton Museum*

Two small portraits of Audie Murphy taken during the war, probably on one of his trips to Paris.
*Source: Audie Murphy/American Cotton Museum*

With sister Corinne Murphy Burns in Farmersville, Texas, June 1945.
*Source: Audie Murphy/American Cotton Museum*

Audie Murphy waves to the crowd in a parade in Corsicana, Texas, summer 1945.
*Source: Audie Murphy/American Cotton Museum*

Murphy signing an autograph for a wounded young veteran at the Army's Ashburn General Hospital in McKinney, Texas, summer 1945.
*Source: Audie Murphy/American Cotton Museum*

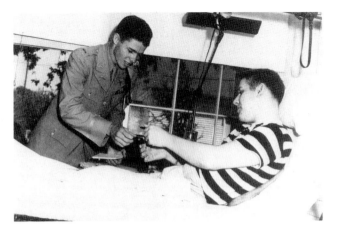

Meeting excited admirers, Corsicana, Texas, summer 1945.
*Source: Audie Murphy/American Cotton Museum*

A serious-faced Audie Murphy being inducted into the Dallas chapter of the Veterans of Foreign Wars, July 1945.
*Source: Audie Murphy/American Cotton Museum*

During a trip to France in 1948, Audie Murphy receives the Legion of Honor and a second Croix de Guerre in a formal ceremony.
*Source: Audie Murphy/American Cotton Museum*

Murphy and first wife Wanda Hendrix posing at a piano, early 1950s.
*Source: Audie Murphy/American Cotton Museum*

Murphy, Bill Mauldin, and John Dierkes in a scene from *The Red Badge of Courage*, MGM Studios, 1951.
*Source: Audie Murphy/American Cotton Museum*

With Pamela Murphy and son Terry during the filming of Universal-International's *To Hell and Back*, fall 1954.
*Source: Audie Murphy/American Cotton Museum*

Helping one of his sons take a drink from a hose on the ranch in Arizona, mid-1950s.
*Source: Audie Murphy/American Cotton Museum*

Blowing out the candles on birthday cakes for sons Terry and James, mid-1950s.
*Source: Audie Murphy/American Cotton Museum*

Audie Murphy oversees the induction of new members of the U.S. Army's "Audie Murphy Platoon" during a publicity appearance in San Antonio, Texas, 1955.
*Source: Audie Murphy/American Cotton Museum*

Murphy's 1955 appearance in San Antonio for the premiere of *To Hell and Back* coincided with the birthday of Davy Crockett. Here he cuts a cake in front of the Alamo.
*Source: Audie Murphy/American Cotton Museum*

James Stewart and Audie Murphy relax during a break in the shooting for Universal-International's *Night Passage*, fall 1956.
*Source: Audie Murphy/American Cotton Museum*

Murphy signing autographs in a Greenville pharmacy, late 1950s or early 1960s.
*Source: Audie Murphy/American Cotton Museum*

On a 1957 press junket for *Night Passage*, Murphy is welcomed at the Denver train station by a crowd of fans.
*Source: Audie Murphy/American Cotton Museum*

Audrey Hepburn as Rachel Zachary, Audie Murphy as Cash Zachary, in a still from *The Unforgiven,* United Artists, 1960.
*Source: Audie Murphy/American Cotton Museum*

Murphy riding his horse Apache Agent in an owner-trainer race in 1963. He finished in first place.
*Source: Audie Murphy/American Cotton Museum*

One of Audie Murphy's last professional publicity photos, late 1960s–early 1970s.
*Source: Audie Murphy/American Cotton Museum*

Soldier"—finally came down to Marshall Thompson, who the studio wanted, and Audie Murphy, whom Huston wanted. Murphy won the role the first week of August. Hedda Hopper in the *LA Times* called Audie's hiring for the movie "the happiest and most appropriate casting of the year." Her lobbying, she thought, had paid off handsomely. "For a change, we'll have a real soldier playing a real soldier on the screen. It couldn't happen at a better time." Rehearsals began three weeks later.[15]

Huston shot a few of the scenes, including the opening river crossing, in northern California near the town of Chico, but the bulk of the filming took place on Huston's own ranch in the San Fernando Valley near Los Angeles. The movie's budget of $1.6 million was nearly three times what any of Murphy's movies had cost before and it was clearly the biggest production of which he had ever been a part. Huston spent hours working with Murphy on how to project emotion, how to move on camera, and how to live the role he was playing. "Everything John Huston suggested to him, he did; there was no arguing or fighting," remembered one of the supporting actors on the set. "Audie had great confidence in John Huston." And Huston believed in Murphy's talent. He just had to find a way to bring it to the surface. "Audie is afraid of making a fool out of himself in front of the camera," Huston later explained. "So he tightens up. I assure him that I'll protect him. He believes me and gives his all."[16]

Huston thought Murphy had star quality. "The screen exaggerates and magnifies whatever it is that a great actor has," Huston said. "It's almost as though greatness is a matter of quality rather than ability. Dad [Walter Huston] had it. He had that something that people felt in him. You sense it every time you're near it." And now he was in its presence again: "You see it in Audie Murphy's eyes. It's like a great horse. You go past his stall and you can feel the vibration in there."[17]

Other executives associated with the movie were openly skeptical of what Huston saw in Murphy and were worried about his well-publicized tendency toward violence. Reinhardt flatly told the director that Murphy would need his "constant attention" and that "he shouldn't be left alone for a single second."[18]

Even with Huston's attentiveness, Murphy was more withdrawn than any actor the director had worked with. Journalist Lillian Ross noted that Huston had to speak to Murphy as if he were trying to comfort a frightened child. "Hello, Audie. How are you, Audie?" When Murphy's interest in the project seemed to flag, Huston invited him to bring his horse out to the ranch and board him there while they were shooting. "You can have your colt right there with you," he said, hoping to comfort him, and he could go off riding by himself at any time he wanted to while they were shooting the picture.[19]

In meetings in the director's office, Murphy often did little more than sit and look sadly out the window. He was usually disengaged from the conversation even if it involved him in some way. "Seems as though nothing can get me excited any more—you know, enthused? Before the war, I'd get excited and enthused about a lot of things, but not any more." Huston spoke as if he were fascinated by Audie Murphy, whom he called a "little, gentle-eyed creature," and, another time, "a gentle little killer."[20]

Many of the actors on the film enjoyed meeting Murphy, about whom they had heard so much, and often they related their surprise at how normal he seemed, given his fame and the honors he had won in the war. "He was just a very nice, very down to earth kind of guy," said Robert Easton. "I liked him immediately." Murphy also impressed his fellow actors with his determination and hard work. Royal Dano, who played a character called the "Tattered Soldier," saw traces of the real soldier in Murphy as he played his part. When they were filming scenes in which they were charging up or down hills, Dano marveled at how Murphy could run at full speed completely doubled over. "He could run so close to the ground that he'd make a damn difficult target," he said. He was also touched by Murphy's subtle kindness. Dano didn't know it, but in the final editing his death scene was cut. When Murphy learned of the cut he drove to Dano's house and broke the news to him and his wife. That was certainly not Murphy's responsibility, and Dano was very moved. It was "a hell of a nice thing to do," he said later. "Audie went out of his way to break it gently for us. That shows a side of Murph you don't usually get from the newspapers and things."[21]

And then there was Murphy's intense pride. In one scene his character was supposed to admit that he was deathly scared during the fighting, but Murphy found the very idea of such a confession repellent. "I can't do it," he said. "I just can't confess a thing like that to this rear-echelon ink-slinger [Bill Mauldin]." Mauldin came up with a possible solution, which was that Murphy's character would admit his fear only after Mauldin's character had confessed to running away. Even acting the part of a coward was difficult for a man who was every day still carrying the burden of being the most decorated soldier in U.S. history.[22]

Mauldin, given his own war experience, understood Murphy better than most. "My furies weren't as burning as his," the cartoonist said, "and I was able to work most of them out on paper. Audie took the hard way, cutting a swath through the Wehrmacht and then trying to do the same in Hollywood." Mauldin was not puzzled by Murphy's actions; he just knew that Murphy was different than most people, and different certainly than most people in Hollywood: "We adjust, accept, tolerate, temporize and sometimes compromise. Not Murphy."

Murphy's performance in *The Red Badge of Courage* was praised in a way that few of his performances were—in fact, the closest comparable praise was for his performance in another movie with John Huston, *The Unforgiven*, in 1960.

Audie Murphy could rarely lose himself in a movie role. "I can't make believe worth a zinc cent," he remarked. He abhorred phoniness, and could never forget that he was reciting lines that someone else had written for him. At the heart of most of the criticism directed at his movie work was the fact that he almost always looked like he was acting. The only way he could usually get through the experience was with the "grim determination" that one critic labeled as his one dependable expression.

Very much like the character of Holden Caulfield in J. D. Salinger's novel *The Catcher in the Rye* that came out the same year as *The Red Badge of Courage*, Audie Murphy could not abide phonies, and that dislike extended even to himself. He had no interest in pretending to be something that he was not, and this was the key reason that he steadfastly refused to play the Hollywood game of glad-handing and back-slapping. It was one of the reasons that he could not want to pretend to like people whom he did not. And it was one of the reasons that his marriage to Wanda Hendrix was doomed to failure. And it lurked in the background of all his attempts to be an actor.[23]

But there was something else too, something that could occasionally offset all these qualities. Murphy proudly was who he was, and when he was asked to play characters with similar virtues, he could, almost despite himself, give a reasonably convincing performance. When a film required him to portray something with which he was familiar, he could call upon reserves of experience and emotion to bring back to life situations he had experienced before. In those instances one could accurately say he was reenacting, not simply acting. That was the case with *The Red Badge of Courage*. That was obviously the case with the film version of *To Hell and Back*. And there were flashes of it in other film roles.[24]

As for the film itself, it seemed to have all the makings of a disaster. Executives at MGM were disappointed at how poorly the test audience reacted to the first screening. Many walked out; others said they were confused by the apparent lack of plot and relative dearth of action. The studio insisted on drastic edits, cutting the film to a brief seventy minutes even after adding on narration by James Whitmore and a prologue assuring the audience that the film was adapted from a classic of American literature. Huston did not stick around to defend his movie, and the unorthodox way in which he had shot it, with disorienting camera angles that was supposed to mimic the experience of being on a battlefield. Huston went on to his next movie, *The African Queen*, part of which would be shot in Africa, and left *The Red Badge of Courage* to the not-so-tender mercies of the studio. Studio executives thought the movie plotless and confusing—and by some standard perhaps they were right. The film was one of the studio's biggest money losers of the year, which meant that however good Murphy's performance had been, it was discounted for having been made in a commercial turkey. As one writer has noted, "The possibility of Murphy gaining recognition as a serious actor was nullified by MGM's handling of *The Red Badge of Courage*." Whether he would get another chance to be so recognized was an open question.[25]

There were rumors that Murphy was giving serious consideration to leaving Hollywood altogether; there were also rumors that he might fight in the Korean War, which had begun in the summer of 1950. He joined the Texas National Guard's 36th Division, the unit that had fought alongside his 3rd Division in the invasion of southern France in 1945. "I think World War III has already started," Murphy solemnly announced at Camp Mabry in Austin, headquarters of the 36th, "and I want to get all the training I can."[26]

He passed his physical exam, but poking a finger at his stomach, he joked, "I suppose I've been in Hollywood a little too long. I'm a little fat and soft." He also, for the first time in public, admitted that he had falsified his birth date for his original Army enlistment in 1942. "The doctor back home couldn't remember exactly when I was born," he said with a smile, "so I was 18." After he was sworn in, he went to Farmersville for the weekend before returning to Hollywood and his movie commitments.[27]

But the Army knew a good thing when they had it handed to them and the idea of using the most famous soldier from World War II—who now also just happened to be a movie star—to boost morale, recruitment, and public support was too good to pass up. Murphy received the rank of captain and took part in divisional maneuvers at Fort Hood in central Texas. He drilled soldiers, marched with them in parade, hiked with them in the field exercises, and bunked down with the other officers. They treated him like any other soldier, and he loved it. "I think today's army is better" than the one in which he had served, he said. The soldiers might be younger (although certainly no younger than he himself had been in World War II), but there were plenty of officers and NCO's "to give them the know-how. That's what we didn't have in the last war—enough leaders with experience." In September 1951 he completed two weeks of active duty with the 36th on maneuvers at Camp Polk in Louisiana where he taught the basics to new infantrymen. He returned to Fort Hood again the following summer to again help train new recruits.[28]

----

He also showed an interest in recruiting female companionship. A few actresses caught his eye. *Variety* said that Murphy and an attractive woman named Peggy Castle were a "random tandem," though a month later it had to acknowledge that the two were "no longer a twittering twain." Universal-International signed Castle to a contract at the suggestion of Murphy, which perhaps says a little more about how close they were.

A writer for the *Saturday Evening Post* speculated that Murphy had not so much "sex appeal as sympathy appeal," and it is true that women often saw, or thought they saw, a vulnerable side to him. "Few women could resist him," David McClure commented. "They all seemed to want to mother him." Murphy was not above using that as an easy avenue to intimacy. "Audie liked girls," said his sometime costar and poker-playing friend Jack Elam. "I mean Audie *really* liked the girls." David McClure said that with each new girl Murphy pursued he seemed to develop a "flaming passion for a few days" or sometimes even a few weeks. But then he would drop them cold.

The skirt-chasing ended when Murphy met Pamela Archer, a hostess supervisor for Braniff airline, who had a crush on Audie Murphy, and the luck to be introduced to him by a Braniff pilot who was a mutual friend. They had dinner together in California when she was out for a visit and soon Murphy was smitten. "The first time I saw her I was a goner," he told a writer for *Modern Screen* magazine. "I wasn't in the market for another wife, or for love." But every time he looked at Pam, he said, he felt wonderful. Archer was quiet, reserved, and interested in having a home life and a family rather than attending Hollywood parties; she was a much better match for Murphy than Wanda Hendrix had been. They talked on the phone constantly and he saw her when he returned to Texas. He "missed her like blazes" when he was off shooting *The Red Badge of Courage*. He called her "Little Squaw" because of her dark hair and dark eyes.[29]

The two were married on April 23, 1951, in a small service at the Highland Park Methodist Church in Dallas, four days after his divorce from Wanda Hendrix was finalized. Murphy asked the chaplain of the 36th Division to officiate the ceremony. James Cherry, the man who had introduced him to show business back in the summer of 1945, served as his best man. As he had done with Wanda Hendrix, Murphy and his new bride spent their honeymoon in Texas, even staying in some of the same places. On their wedding night, Murphy leapt from the bed with his pistol when he saw a prowler lurking outside their motel room window. Pamela screamed for her husband not to shoot, and the prowler ran away.

---

After *The Red Badge of Courage*, Audie Murphy was back at Universal making westerns, starting with *The Cimarron Kid*, which began filming in the spring of 1951. His new bride came with him for the location shooting in Sonora, California. Though it was a low budget film (less than $500,000), Murphy earned $15,000 for his performance, his biggest paycheck yet. The ability that he had shown in his previous work was, as one critic noted, "conspicuous by its absence," but Murphy was well aware of his limitations as an actor, and knew that galloping horses, dusty chases, and exciting gunfights best suited his talents. "Sure I like making westerns," he said. "I'm one actor who isn't hankering to play Hamlet—unless I could be Hamlet on horseback." Murphy made seven more westerns in quick succession.[30]

His personal life now seemed remarkably stable as well. He and his wife welcomed their first child Terence Michael, named after Murphy's friend Terry Hunt, on March 14, 1952. Murphy relaxed by going fishing and hunting, got involved with raising quarter horses, and was the doting father who took his son with him to movie locations. A second son, whom they named James in honor of James Cherry, was born almost exactly two years after his first. Audie even remarked to a fan magazine that his nightmares of the war "were gradually diminishing and will probably disappear entirely." To an outside observer it seemed as though the nation's most decorated soldier was finally starting to live the kind of life he deserved.

CHAPTER TEN

# TO HELL AND BACK

I n the middle of the 1950s Audie Murphy was one of the most
popular stars in Hollywood. During those years he regularly
received more than 600 fan letters a month and moviegoers
ranked him among the top ten favorite actors year in and year out,
putting him in the company of stars like Doris Day, Elizabeth
Taylor, and Rock Hudson. While some critics still labeled his performances as wooden or emotionally empty, in reality he was beginning
to improve greatly as an actor and delivered solid if low-key and
restrained work. Other critics, however, were coming to appreciate
the qualities he brought to the roles he played. In a review of 1954's
*Ride Clear of Diablo*, *Newsweek* said "it is very difficult for Murphy
to appear unnatural in anything he does, whether it be a first-class
motion picture like *The Red Badge of Courage* or the present routine
job." In general, he was growing comfortable with being an actor.
"I'm as happy working in pictures as I would be in any other business,"

he said. "There are things I don't like and people I don't like, but that would be true whether I worked for the movies or the telephone company or anything else." Even his closest friend, David McClure, thought Murphy was happier now than he had ever seen him.[1]

In the 1950s, movie stars were expected to travel throughout the country to attend the openings of their movies, and this made fans feel even closer and more emotionally invested in their favorite stars. In contrast to the way things were in later years, film premieres took place not just in Los Angeles and New York but in smaller cities like Dallas, Kansas City, Seattle, even Great Falls, Montana. For the stars this meant a long succession of hotel rooms, interviews, and public appearances. Because of his high profile, Audie Murphy usually had a hotel suite to himself rather than just a single or even shared room when he embarked on these tours. But he was no egotistical star; in fact, his natural humility and self-effacement always came across as refreshingly charming, reinforcing his all-American image. "Whenever or wherever he appears, he is a perfect gentleman," said Frank McFadden, one of Universal's publicity managers who became a friend of Murphy's and often accompanied him on these press junkets.

In Kansas City on the supporting tour for *The Cimarron Kid*, the superintendent of the city public school system asked if Murphy could stay in the city a little longer, and if so, would he agree to a special appearance just for the students. He was always responsive to what he thought was a good cause, especially involving children. "Although he is not a great orator, he delivers his lines in such a sincere and forthright manner that he is quite reminiscent of a young Will Rogers."

In late May 1953, during the break between filming *Tumbleweed* and *Ride Clear of Diablo*, Audie Murphy went to Dallas to emcee a show at the Palace Theater to benefit victims of a tornado that had devastated the city of Waco earlier in the month, killing 114 people. Murphy, Gene Autry, and others took part in a stage show featuring local music groups and the theater screened Murphy's latest release *Gunsmoke*. That night the Palace raised $4,600. Interstate Theaters all around the Dallas area collected donations that night as well.[2]

But as he travelled from city to city with Murphy, Frank McFadden became aware of things that the general public never saw. One night there was a mix-up in the hotel reservations and the travelling company all had to share rooms. He and Murphy bunked together in a double. When Murphy took off his sport coat in the room that evening, it was the first time McFadden realized that he always carried a gun with him. He watched as Murphy took the gun, a small revolver, out of its holster and slipped it under the pillow on his bed.

About two in the morning, McFadden was abruptly awakened by a terrible racket. To his shock, Murphy was up and pounding the wall next to his bed with his fists so hard they were starting to bleed, but he remained sound asleep. He gently tried to wake him up by repeatedly calling his name and Murphy slowly came to his senses. Without a word he went into the bathroom and washed the blood from his hands. "I had a dream," he said simply, when he reemerged, and got back into his bed and went to sleep.

McFadden was deeply shaken by the experience. While they remained friends and continued to travel together and work with each other after that night, he never slept in the same room with him again. When the cavalcade rolled into Dallas, the two took a break from the schedule of appearances and went hunting on some land owned by a friend of Murphy's. Only there did he seem to relax noticeably and genuinely enjoy himself. "He was happy on a ranch when he was around ranch people," McFadden concluded. "That's when he was really Audie."[3]

Once when one of his movie junkets was passing through Dallas, McFadden encountered an older man loitering in the lobby of the Adolphus Hotel asking about Audie Murphy. He claimed to be Murphy's father and was hoping to see him. McFadden went upstairs and dutifully reported the news to Murphy. "I don't have a father," was his only reply. The man went away.[4]

Professionally, Audie Murphy was building a solid reputation as a reliable actor for westerns. Nathan Juran, who directed Murphy in *Gunsmoke, Tumbleweed,* and *Drums Across the River,* three of the five movies he made in rapid succession between the summer of 1952 and October 1953, said that Murphy was a "sure-shot guy." He could not remember him ever flubbing his lines or making a mistake. For these B movies, Juran explained, "an 18-day shooting schedule was considered generous," and the low budgets precluded continual retakes. Murphy's fellow B-movie fixture Ronald Reagan joked that producers of these movies "didn't want them good, they wanted them Thursday." An actor who could dependably hit his marks and deliver his lines the first time was one worth having around.[5]

While he came to be on friendly terms with many of his costars, Murphy did not often socialize with them. Very few of them did he consider to be his friends and he had very little interest in pretending otherwise. Instead, during location shoots he usually spent most of his free time with the men of the crew, the stuntmen, and the wranglers who took care of the horses. He felt comfortable in their company; they were his sort of people. He joked with them, told stories, twirled pistols and occasionally showed off his shooting skills; and, just as he had with his buddies in the Army, Murphy gambled.

Gambling was incessant on any film set when Audie Murphy was around—whether for large or small stakes depended on whom he was playing with. Sometimes he would stand over a group of men who were throwing a game of dice, and drop down hundred-dollar bill after hundred-dollar bill, with nothing more than saying "cover it." When it came to cards, poker and gin were the games he played most often, and he had the reputation of always raising the stakes and demanding his money immediately whenever he won. But he also had a reputation for scrupulous honesty. "Audie was a gambler who wouldn't cheat," said fellow actor Jack Elam, himself regarded as one of the best card players in town, and one of Murphy's closest friends in the business. Elam often played poker with Murphy using only hundred-dollar-bills, which, when they played in the studio commissary, always drew a crowd of astonished spectators. But almost every time Murphy was at the card table, it seemed as though his luck simply abandoned him. John Huston, in fact, thought he was probably the most unlucky gambler he had ever met. "Always unlucky," he said, "*always*. Not unskilled, just unlucky."[6]

Since he had come to Hollywood, Murphy had also bet prodigiously on horse races. Elam in fact had first met him through a bookie who operated out of a gas station during the time Murphy was still under contract to Cagney Productions. By the time they were costars together, Murphy was betting on the horses for much higher stakes than when he was just playing cards with his buddies. He always bet on a horse to win, never merely to place or show, and the higher the bet the more he seemed to like it. "He'd as soon bet $200,000 on a horse as he would $20," said a stuntman with whom Murphy became friends and track buddies. "Money had no home with Audie."[7]

You knew you were one of his friends, said another, if he took you to the track with him. When he could not find horse races in southern California, he would gather a few friends and go across the border to Tijuana, Mexico. The wild scene there captivated him. One time he even took Pamela, along with a few other Hollywood couples, to a bullfight.[8]

It seemed as though the gambling, the horse racing, and all the rest were risks Audie Murphy took to inject excitement into his life, either to rejuvenate his war-dulled senses or recover that heightened sense of experience that came from the stresses of war. In the wake of experiencing combat, as he had admitted to John Huston, nothing excited him. But that did not keep him from continually searching for something that could make him feel alive. He once called Hollywood the "dullest town in the world," and because of that, he reasoned, he started betting on the horses. "I got so that four hundred dollars was a minimum bet. Even that was boring," he admitted, "I didn't care if I won or lost." Eventually this led to more than just what would be considered "traditional" gambling; he began to take business risks. At one point in the 1950s, he and Terry Hunt worked up a plan to open a nationwide chain of health clubs. Another time he was determined to go into the business of breeding quarter horses. "He seemed to have no interest in solid business ventures," McClure said. "He wanted to deal in risks! If the risks paid off, the income would be great. If the risks didn't pay off, Audie would just shrug and go on to some other crazy business." It was another symptom of his mental combat trauma, just as was the insomnia, the nightmares harrowing and vivid enough to have him punching the walls in his sleep, and the compulsion to have his gun with him at all times. The other risk he allegedly took was cheating on his wife.[9]

"How ya' gonna keep 'em down on the farm after they've seen Paree?" asked one of the hit songs that came out of the First World War. It was a playful tune with a gloss of innocence, but it hinted at a grim truth about any war for those who fought in it. Taking part in combat was a fundamental divide in the lives of soldiers, and they returned to their previous lives changed in ways that were sometimes not immediately visible to those who stayed behind. Audie Murphy was not one to make excuses, but he blamed some of his behavior on the experience of war. "War robs you mentally and physically," he said with clinical detachment. "It drains you. Things don't thrill you any more. It's a struggle every day to find something interesting to do."[10]

"After two or three years of combat it does something to you," he added, but "it takes a while to realize what it has done to you." He thought the Army, which he otherwise loved, should have done more to help veterans readjust to civilian life. "Our war dogs were detrained after the war," he said, "but not the soldiers."

Even if he gambled incessantly, made risky investments, had money hidden away to finance his affairs, and was unmindful about saving money, Murphy did not live extravagantly. In fact, he took pride in living modestly, without Hollywood ostentation. He had a comfortable house, but no swimming pool. The fan magazines reported that he turned his checkbook over to his wife with the confession, "I'm too impulsive. Pam's more logical, so she takes care of keeping us on the beam financially."[11]

It was excitement, not materialism, that drove him. Through his friend Frank Hronek, a detective with the Los Angeles Police Department, Murphy started going on nighttime ride-alongs with the LAPD. When he was in Texas, where Dallas County sheriff Bill Decker had appointed him an honorary deputy, he often did the same thing with the Dallas police. Indeed, he tried to cultivate such relationships with police and sheriffs' departments across the country. In the spring of 1956, when he was in Tucson filming a movie, he took part in an undercover narcotics operation with the Pima County sheriff's department, walking the streets of the city at night, unarmed, posing as a drug buyer. His participation resulted in several arrests both there and in Houston where he did the same thing. He was a "first rate agent," said one member of the Tucson police, and he was motivated by a "deep hatred for drug dealers." Murphy himself said that he did such an unexpected thing "because I am interested, as every citizen should be, in stamping out the narcotics traffic and combatting juvenile delinquency." What he did not explain, however, was that this was a way for him to feel the excitement of combat again. His life had become a fight "to keep from being bored to death. That's what two years of combat did to me!" He spent his years trying to feel the rush that came from putting his life on the line, which nothing else he had found since had been able to equal.[12]

Gradually, the executives at Universal-International began talking more and more about the project in which everyone had an interest—everyone that is, except Audie Murphy himself. Since the publication of *To Hell and Back*, people at the studio knew it was just a matter of time until they brought Murphy's wartime story to the screen. U-I secured the movie rights to the book in 1950 but nothing had happened since. Things finally started to come together in late 1953 after filming wrapped up on *Drums Across the River*. Late in December, Universal announced that it had signed Jesse Hibbs to direct a film version of *To Hell and Back* and that the project would begin the following spring. Hibbs was a long-time assistant director with the studio and directed Murphy in the well-received *Ride Clear of Diablo*. Since then he had also directed three more formulaic westerns for U-I.[13]

At first, Murphy had no interest in playing himself in the movie. He had lived through it all when it happened the first time, and then had to revisit it all to write the book. He wanted nothing more to do with those events. In writing the book in the first place he had been determined that it would not come across as only *his* story about *his* medals. In this, he and McClure had been notably successful, producing a book that was a heartfelt testament to his fellow combat veterans. Knowing well how Hollywood told its stories, Murphy was convinced a movie would inevitably put the focus back on him. In the book he had not even mentioned his medals; what was the chance that the studio would allow a movie to ignore them? His tone, in discussing the project, turned bitter. "It was a lousy book because it was a lousy war," he grumbled. He suggested that if it had to be made, maybe Tony Curtis—whom he personally disliked—would be a good fit to play the lead.[14]

But his friends rallied round, urging him to do it, that he *had* to do it if the movie was going to be made at all. He continued to resist, fearing it would come across as vainglorious or, as he put it, "self-eulogizing." At last, it was Frank McFadden who convinced him. "Nobody can portray you better than you can," he said. It was hard to argue with that.[15]

Once Murphy was onboard with the project, he and director Jesse Hibbs began talking at length about how best to bring the story to the screen. Hibbs found Murphy extremely reluctant to talk about any of the events of his life, from his childhood to his war experiences. The studio hired the talented screenwriter Gil Doud to try to open Murphy up, particularly about his childhood. But he did not want to talk about it—or even remember it.

Murphy, Hibbs, Doud, and producer Aaron Rosenberg finally worked their way through a script, but Murphy remained doubtful of how certain events would come across on film. He had reason to be skeptical. Studio executives were already worried that the overall tone of the book was far too glum to make into a successful and crowd-pleasing movie. It was much too full of "hate, frustration, horror, futile courage and terror." To be a real moneymaker they believed it needed more uplifting material, more humor, "and a more encouraging conclusion." It needed to be cleaned up.[16]

Determined to exert more influence over this film than any of his previous ones, Murphy got involved with the production to a degree he never had before. In addition to working with the script, he also took part in the decisions over casting the movie. It was he who chose Charles Drake for the important role of Lattie Tipton, who, as in the book, would go by the name of Brandon. Drake was a veteran actor who was eight years older than Murphy and had been making movies since 1941. Early in his career he had uncredited roles in *Sergeant York* and James Cagney's *Yankee Doodle Dandy*. More recently he had moved into westerns, including a part in Murphy's own *Gunsmoke*. Murphy liked him, and even said that Drake exuded the same quiet dependability that Tipton himself had possessed. Murphy also cast his own son Terry as one of his little brothers in the family history scenes.

In the one film he had made with Murphy before *To Hell and Back*, and then in several subsequent movies they made together, director Jesse Hibbs found that Murphy usually never commented on the script or took much of an interest in the details. He just "did exactly as he was told." Not now. Now he was "tenacious about every point." As a measure of how determined he was to make this movie reflect the truth, he also acted as a technical advisor for the film, getting involved in a myriad of little details to ensure the film's accuracy. "No Hollywood hero has ever had as much technical say-so about a film as Audie Murphy," noted *Life* magazine. He even got down into the shell holes that the crew had dug and showed the prop men how to paint the dirt so it would look scorched from an explosion. "This was one movie I wanted to see done right if at all," he explained. "I didn't want to low-budget the 3rd Division." The producers also recruited Colonel Michael Paulick, whom Murphy had once rescued during the fighting around the quarry in the Vosges Mountains, as a second technical advisor.[17]

To reinforce the narrative focus on the men with whom Murphy fought, and to remind viewers that they were seeing far more than the story of just one soldier, however heroic, the film's producers agreed to include a prologue delivered by General Walter Bedell Smith, who during the war had been Eisenhower's Chief of Staff. "The story you are about to see is theirs," Smith reads stiffly for the rolling camera, "the true story of the foot soldier as seen through the eyes of one of them, Audie L. Murphy."

The shooting for the movie began at Fort Lewis, Washington, in September, 1954. Enthused about the project and hoping that it would portray the Army in a positive light, the Army provided the filmmakers with vehicles, tanks, artillery pieces, and the use of the entire 44th Infantry Division as extras. Because of the shooting schedule, the battle atop the tank destroyer at Holtzwihr would not be filmed in the snow, as it really took place, but most of the combat scenes reflected the terrain of Sicily, Italy, and southern France well enough, even if there was never enough mud.

But it was Murphy's performance, many critics agreed, that separated the movie from the other formulaic combat fare of the late 1940s and 1950s. Valor had been portrayed on the big screen more dramatically, said the *New York Times*, but Murphy's performance gave "stature, credibility and dignity to an autobiography that would be routine and hackneyed without him." His tendency to underact served him better in this film than in his previous ones. "One is rarely conscious that the small, self-effacing GI with the slow drawl is simply acting out feats of extraordinary bravery."[18]

Murphy's overall performance was his best simply because it was his most natural. His salutes to superior officers were crisp. His movements in the field were precise and self-assured. His exhortations for his men to get up and follow him seemed real, not lines in a script.

There are scenes, however, that seem almost cruel to inflict on a man so traumatized by the experience of war. Studio executives rationalized that by acting out the scenes of his mother's death, Lattie Tipton's death, and the general horror of combat, Murphy could somehow exorcise his demons. Tipton's death scene was the toughest for Murphy and he found repeated excuses to postpone shooting it. Murphy admitted that the battle scenes made him uneasy. It was like "when your mind plays back something that you don't want to hear or see or feel again." He had spent years holding such memories at bay, only to have them explode in his dreams at night. Reliving these scenes also brought out a lurking sense of guilt. "How else could I feel when most of the men who'd fought beside me never came back, never saw the posthumous medals or big parades, never tasted the bittersweet taste of victory?"[19]

Some of the scenes are pure Hollywood contrivance, such as the bar in North Africa in which men from Murphy's company watch an exotic dancer singing "Dogface Soldier," the song of the 3rd Division. Murphy vehemently disapproved of the ending of the movie in which he is awarded the Medal of Honor and then watches the division parade before him like he was some sort of conquering hero. It was the only scene about which he and Jesse Hibbs could not find a compromise, and the director finally prevailed. Filming wrapped at the end of October 1954.

Universal-International clearly believed it had a potential blockbuster on its hands. In July 1955, it launched the first-ever nationwide television ad campaign for a movie. Ads for *To Hell and Back* appeared on sixty-seven television stations months prior to the picture's scheduled release. The studio bought billboard spaces in forty-two markets to publicize the coming big-screen story of the country's most decorated soldier.[20]

*Life* magazine again took up the cause of Audie Murphy. In *To Hell and Back* "Audie is no mere actor," it assured its readers. The jarring battle scenes in the film were the most "effective infantry combat footage to be filmed since the Army Signal Corps filmed the real thing." The magazine published several photo stills from the movie, the captions under which were written as though they were lifted from the war itself, and put the focus squarely where the public wanted it. "Attacking in anger after a friend's death, Murphy single-handedly wipes out an entire German position, using captured gun." The most traumatic event in the life of the most decorated soldier in American history was followed breezily by a Corn Flakes ad.[21]

On July 2, 1955, Audie Murphy left Hollywood for New York City where he kicked off a nationwide tour of appearances in support of *To Hell and Back* months before the movie was scheduled to open. From New York he went to Washington, D.C., where at the Capitol building he was the honored guest of the Texas Congressional delegation. Everyone knew him. Everyone wanted to shake his hand. Staffers poked their heads out of doorways as he walked the marble corridors. Murphy met Vice President Richard Nixon and also testified before a Senate Judiciary subcommittee hearing on juvenile delinquency and explained to the star-struck senators that he had become interested in the subject through the filming of his movie *Bad Boy* and his affiliation with the LAPD. He hoped, he said, to make a movie about the evils of narcotics. The studio arranged for a private invitation-only Washington, D.C., preview of *To Hell and Back*.

The publicity tour for the movie was distinctly reminiscent of the circuit he had made in 1945, including the fact that he was in uniform much of the time. In San Antonio for the world premiere of *To Hell and Back* on August 17 (coinciding with the birthday of Davy Crockett), he led a parade on horseback through downtown before an enthusiastic crowd of 200,000 and laid a wreath at the entrance to the Alamo.

There was a line all day at the box office, forcing an extra showing (Murphy appeared at each one), and the movie broke all attendance records for an opening at a San Antonio theater. At the end of the day he oversaw the induction of fifty enlistees into the army's newest unit, the Audie Murphy Platoon. Then he flew to Houston, where the movie again broke theater records.

When he landed at the Dallas airport the following morning, elements of two army divisions and a drum and bugle corps were there to welcome him, alongside an array of civic leaders and a cheering throng. He made five stage appearances throughout the day at the Majestic Theater, where that night they unveiled a bust of Murphy before the 7:25 showing. "We thought it would do nice business," said Murphy's old friend James Cherry, who managed the Majestic, but the crowds far exceeded expectations. The next day Murphy travelled thirty miles west to Fort Worth where he again was greeted as a conquering hero.[22]

From Texas he travelled to Chicago for four days of press conferences and television appearances. Then he was off to Boston to be the guest of honor at a gala black tie VFW dinner and to be the Grand Marshall of the Boston VFW parade the next day.[23]

"We ascribe the popularity of To Hell and Back entirely to Audie's personality as a screen star," a Dallas newspaper editorialized a week later. "Texans have been patronizing a favorite actor, not a hero." That seems unlikely—especially written about a movie based on Audie Murphy's life story. Texans, like Americans everywhere, still remembered Audie Murphy as the most decorated soldier in American history; that fact, not any screen performance, was his real claim to fame. It was also telling that Murphy's popularity, and the film's, was, in the estimation of the paper, greatest with "adults from forty to eighty and the kids from six to about sixteen." Missing were young adults "who, for one reason or another, have escaped Audie's charms. Maybe he will get them later."[24] Another way of looking at it was that veterans his own age did not need to be reminded about the war; and to those in their twenties who had missed the war, he already represented an older generation.

To Hell and Back was a smash hit. Redbook magazine selected it as its Picture of the Month for September and by October it was the top movie in the country. Variety estimated that Murphy would earn at least $500,000 from the project. By spring 1956, To Hell and Back had earned more than $6 million. The studio began to talk about a sequel, signed Hibbs to direct, and approached David McClure to write it. Executives planned for it to be titled The Way Back and it would follow Murphy as he readjusted to postwar life outside the army. If the script reflected Audie Murphy's real experience, it would have been a grim movie indeed, hardly the triumphant story that studio executives wanted to imagine. But the project never gained serious traction beyond McClure writing some notes for a book he thought he would call Helmets in the Dust. A few years later, Murphy bought the rights to any sequel of To Hell and Back and no such movie was ever made.[25]

Audie Murphy made more money from To Hell and Back than from any other single film in which he was involved. He received 60 percent of the movie rights from the book, $100,000 for his acting and role as technical advisor, and 10 percent of the film's total net profits. He used some of his windfall to purchase a ninety-acre farm near Dallas (which he nevertheless turned around and sold within a month, making a profit of about $25,000) and an 841-acre ranch in Riverside County, California, where he began raising and selling quarter horses. He also bought a working cattle ranch of 16,000 acres about thirty miles southeast of Tucson, which he christened the "TM Ranch," after his son's initials.[26]

Universal-International now had to consider whether they had a full-fledged major star on their hands rather than simply a popular B-movie cowboy actor. His first film in the wake of the success of *To Hell and Back* was *World in My Corner*, where he was cast as a determined prizefighter, and again teamed him with director Jesse Hibbs and producer Aaron Rosenberg. Murphy took the part seriously and trained hard at Terry Hunt's gym. He wanted to look like a real boxer when he was in the ring, not just some phony actor who was pretending. "He's the first actor I ever saw who wasn't afraid of getting hit hard in a prize fight scene," said one of his costars. But the end result was disappointing. A weak and clichéd script along with a predictable plot were simply too much to overcome. For his part, Murphy understood the inherent weakness of the film all too well. "People can sit home and see four or five fights a week on TV. Why would they go to the movies to see a phony fight and a skimpy story?"[27]

In September 1955, flush with martial enthusiasm from *To Hell and Back*, Audie Murphy purchased a story about the Air Force Survival School. He wanted to make it into a movie starring himself, and it was the first indication that he wanted to take more control of his projects and perhaps double as a producer.[28]

Before the end of the year he formed the "Audie Murphy Company," teaming with established producer Harry Joe Brown. In 1956 he acquired the options on Thames Williamson's highly regarded 1933 novel *The Wood's Colt*, and C. William Harrison's short story *The Petticoat Brigade*. He and Brown developed the latter into a film called *The Guns of Fort Petticoat* that went before the camera in Old

Tucson with Murphy in the lead role of a cavalry lieutenant who transforms a group of women into a fighting force. During the filming, Murphy's ulcers flared up and he had to return to Los Angeles for emergency surgery. The movie was poorly received and Murphy and Brown parted ways amidst lawsuits and acrimony. In the fall of 1958 Murphy was sued again, this time by a writer named Paul Kazear who claimed that Murphy had commissioned a screenplay from him called "Skindiver with a Heart." He had delivered it on time, said the suit, but had not been paid.[29]

Murphy missed several opportunities to broaden his range as an actor or to go deeper into producing. On the production side, he offered MGM half a million dollars for *The Red Badge of Courage*, in hopes of re-editing and re-releasing it, but MGM declined. In 1957, the actor Robert Mitchum wanted Audie Murphy to star in *Thunder Road*, a movie Mitchum was producing (he had also coauthored the script) but Murphy was tied up in his own productions. Universal, meanwhile, wanted to cast him in a film based on the life of American western painter Charles Russell, again pairing him with Hibbs. But impending early snows around Great Falls, Montana, where they were going to shoot the film forced the project's postponement and eventual cancelation. Instead, Murphy was cast in another safe and predictable western *Walk the Proud Land*.[30]

In the summer of 1956, the studio put Murphy in an ill-fitting and far-fetched comedy called *Joe Butterfly* about American soldiers in occupied Japan, where the film was shot on location. The film costarred Burgess Meredith as the Japanese "Joe Butterfly," apparently only because he had played a similar role on Broadway in *Teahouse of the August Moon*. Murphy was uncomfortable with his role in the film. For any comedy, one critic noted sarcastically, it bodes ill when nobody says anything funny. One of the screenwriters agreed, though he shifted the blame to one of the stars, saying, "Audie shouldn't have been playing comedy." Murphy took home $51,000 for his part, but at the theaters it was another flop.[31]

Not only were the critics giving his films a beating, his body was taking one too. His most serious ailment had been recurring stomach ulcers. While shooting *Walk the Proud Land* (and helping the Tucson police catch drug dealers) he had a bad bout of strep throat. He also got sick on location in Durango, Colorado, during the filming of *Night Passage*. That movie, however, had a $1.6 million budget, which allowed for retakes when necessary. [32]

*Night Passage* became the biggest hit Audie Murphy was involved in since *To Hell and Back*, and gave an indication of what kind of impression he could make on an audience if he did not have to carry a picture all by himself. The movie starred Jimmy Stewart, fresh from shooting *The Spirit of St. Louis* for Warner Brothers. In *Night Passage*, released in 1957, Stewart had the top billing while Murphy, who played his younger brother, did not even appear on screen until half an hour into the action. Costar Dianne Foster believed that Murphy enjoyed working with someone of Stewart's stature and temperament but, as usual, he spent most of his free time playing cards with the crew, except during the time his wife and children joined him on the set. Murphy was a limited actor, Foster noted, but "he was believable because he had an honesty to him and he projected that honesty on the screen." In the right part, in the right production, with a good script, he did just that.

Murphy seemed to get another break when Academy Award-winning director Joseph L. Mankiewicz insisted on casting Murphy in his film version of Graham Greene's novel *The Quiet American*. Mankiewicz, who wrote the screenplay, said Murphy was "the perfect symbol of what I want to say." Indeed, Greene's descriptions in the novel of the title character as having an "unmistakably young and unused face," and who "seemed incapable of harm" sounded precisely like Audie Murphy. The director had initially wanted Lawrence Olivier to play the other lead role, but Olivier flatly refused to work with Audie Murphy. Finally Mankiewicz chose veteran English actor Michael Redgrave.[33]

Murphy took the film seriously and understood how different it was from the other movies that he had made and consequently, that it was a serious opportunity for his career to advance. "I'd be doing myself a favor if I made this one for nothing," he said. Filming began in Saigon, South Vietnam, at the end of January 1957. One weekend early in the shoot Murphy flew to Hong Kong for a weekend and while there, his searing stomach pain became too much to bear. A doctor told him he was suffering from acute appendicitis and emergency surgery was crucial. Rumors were whispered about delays of up to six weeks in filming, but as it had been with Murphy's hospital stays during the war, he wanted nothing more than to be out of bed and back in the action. He recovered remarkably quickly and was back in Saigon in a little over a week, a dozen pounds lighter but eager to resume his role.[34]

Redgrave and Murphy did not get along. Redgrave thought very little of Murphy's ability as an actor and abhorred his affinity for guns, and, as usual, Murphy was armed. The South Vietnamese government was fighting a communist insurgency, and as filming took place as much as seventy-five miles outside of Saigon, Murphy was always on edge. "The commies were only sixteen miles from Saigon at the time, and you never knew what was going to happen," he said. "I figured if they were going to get me, I'd give them a good fight first."[35] U.S. military advisors in South Vietnam gave Murphy a .45 caliber pistol and 500 rounds of ammunition.

By the time filming moved to Rome in the middle of March, Murphy was losing interest in the movie. Pamela came to join her husband, and during a break in the filming, they drove south to Anzio. Unlike his previous trips to his old battlefields, he found Anzio had been much repaired and restored. The sight of the Allied cemetery there affected him tremendously.

The *New York Times* noted that the film version of *The Quiet American* removed much of the "anti-American venom" from the original novel, a change that Graham Greene himself angrily condemned. Its message was still ambiguous, particularly for what the public expected in an Audie Murphy movie. That it was shot in black and white, rather than the now preferred Technicolor, only heightened the suspicion that this was not a mainstream Hollywood offering, nor was it likely to be popular. The movie's appeal would be limited, one critic suggested, because of its difficult plot, and it was "likely that mass audiences will get restless with it." Jan Merlin, an actor who worked with Murphy a few years later said, "I wish the picture would have worked for him because it could have changed what he was doing." Murphy dismissed the film as the "biggest artistic flop of his career."[36]

Whether those mass audiences were restless with Audie Murphy, however, was by no means certain. In the broader public, Murphy's name still carried significant weight with moviegoers. He was only a dozen years from his military fame and an appealing movie star. Despite there being a few artistic misses so far in his Hollywood career, his smash *To Hell and Back* reminded everyone of his unequalled service, his record of heroism, and his box office appeal. When it became widely known that John Wayne was planning a movie about the fall of the Alamo, Murphy's fans, particularly in Texas, were incensed to learn that Wayne was not thinking of casting Murphy in the film. In addition to his war record, Murphy "has turned out to be one of the best outdoor actors in motion pictures," said a writer for the *Dallas Morning News*. In addition to his good looks and "decent skill at dialogue," Murphy had "all the talents Wayne needs for gun and saddle." The paper urged its readers to send letters of support for Audie to Murphy's friend and local Hollywood conduit Bob O'Donnell at the Majestic Theater, and O'Donnell agreed to pass them along to the Duke himself. Despite the public interest, Wayne—who, after all, did not have complete control of the casting decisions—did not press for Murphy to be included in the cast and ultimately he was not.[37]

Nevertheless, Murphy was now something of an American icon. He had a rose named after him (a hybrid developed by a nursery in Oregon) and in the fall of 1956 there was a red-headed burlesque dancer performing in southern California under the name of Audie Murphy. One columnist wrote the perfect tagline: "She isn't wearing enough to pin on his medals!" *Follies* magazine carried a picture of her, which prompted Murphy to quip, "Heck, I never posed for that!" If nothing else, these amusing side notes highlighted that Murphy's status in American culture had not wavered, and whatever his professional disappointments, his career was far from over.[38]

# CHAPTER ELEVEN

# RIDING A CROOKED TRAIL

udie Murphy was well paid for all the movies he made in the late 1950s, but as quickly as the money came in, it just as quickly flowed out. He was still entranced by the excitement of gambling and was spending more time at the racetrack and getting more involved with the business of horse racing. He was now raising racehorses on his ranch near Los Angeles and traveled as far away as Colorado to stable some of them and watch them race. In Denver he met and hired a jockey named Jay Fishburn to ride for him. The two got on well. Murphy was a very easy man to work for, he said, whether you were his jockey or his trainer. "Audie had some good horses that made him a lot of money," Fishburn recalled, but he would bet so much, often thousands and thousands of dollars a day, that he would do well just to break even. "But money had no meaning to Audie," he said. "You couldn't believe how he could go through money."[1]

By the time he made *Ride a Crooked Trail* in September 1957, Audie Murphy's gambling habit was growing noticeably worse. On that set, he met actor Walter Matthau, an avid gambler himself, and the two fed off each other. "They'd bet $2000 to $5000 a card," stuntman Jack Williams said in amazement. "Audie was just absolutely addicted to gambling." When it came to poker, he wanted in on every hand. "Audie wanted action. But in poker you have to sit there and wait. Audie was about instant gratification." It was not about the money. It was his craving for anything that could make him excited, make him feel alive. "With Audie," said one of his costars, "gambling is a matter of living on the edge." For *Ride a Crooked Trail* he was paid $50,000 again, but more ominously, the studio agreed to erase $1,300 he had somehow come to owe it.[2]

Shortly after the shooting for that movie wrapped, Universal was once again pushing Murphy to stretch his acting credentials. Early in 1958 he went to Newport Beach, California, to begin work on *The Gun Runners*, the third filmed variation on an Ernest Hemingway short story called *One Trip Across*. Like *The Quiet American*, the movie had overtones of contemporary politics as it cast Murphy as a fishing boat owner in Key West who becomes entangled in a plot to smuggle guns to Cuban rebels. The director, Don Siegel, who had directed Murphy in 1952's *The Duel at Silver Creek*, thought he was a terrible choice to play the role, particularly considering that Humphrey Bogart had played the same part so distinctively for Howard Hawks in 1944's *To Have and Have Not*, the first time the Hemingway story was made into a movie. Unlike Bogart, Audie Murphy "was incredibly shy and strange and there was a problem reaching him to get a good performance," the director said. When he instructed Murphy and Patricia Owen to rehearse their love scene, Murphy would not touch Owen or even look her in the face. Siegel could not believe it. "She'd caress Audie's face, sit on his lap and attempt to kiss him.

It's hard to believe but I couldn't get any response from Audie. By twisting and turning he managed not to look at her once."[3]

As a director, Siegel appreciated that Murphy did not get drunk, was always on time, knew his lines reasonably well, and did not cause any trouble "as long as you didn't tread on his temper," but such qualities could not automatically rescue a lackluster movie. In many ways *The Gun Runners*, which was released by United Artists in September, the same month that *Ride a Crooked Trail* hit the theaters, was a standard Audie Murphy performance. In a review of his acting ability, typical of the sort that always sought to shine a positive light on his performances, one critic explained that "while it can't be claimed that he helps a dramatic situation, it can be claimed that he never has hurt one." It was faint praise, but perhaps the only kind that the film warranted. As was by now typical, the action sequences were the only time he really appeared to forget that he was acting. He could still summon his charming smile, and in this film he turned in a creditable job of portraying a man who was helplessly aware that he was getting deeper into a situation that was over his head. In playing that kind of part, Murphy was not really acting at all; it was a feeling he knew all too well.[4]

Looking back at his turn as an unwilling gun runner, Audie Murphy said in his typically self-deprecating way that the film had been pretty much like all his other work. "I've done this picture thirty times, only it was with horses instead of boats." The remark was not exactly accurate but reflected his sense that his movies were in large part interchangeable. With the exceptions of *The Red Badge of Courage* and *To Hell and Back*, the significant body of work he had done in westerns was lacking any one film of distinction, any one that could stand apart from the others as great. In late August just before *The Gun Runners* was released, he began filming yet another western, this one entitled *No Name on the Bullet*. As shooting began in the Conejo Valley, just up the coast to the west of Los Angeles, there was little indication that this one would be different from the others. But it turned out to be one of the best movies he ever made.

In the movie, directed by Jack Arnold, Audie Murphy played a famous hired killer named John Gant, who one day appears unexpectedly in a quiet western town. Half of the townspeople think Gant has come for them, and the ensuing movie is tense and psychological, not revealing the identity of his target until the very end of the picture. Murphy's part played to his strengths, and ironically perhaps even to his weaknesses as an actor. The character of John Gant is quiet and withdrawn, a man of few words and fewer emotions. One senses much tension beneath the cool demeanor. His business is simply killing, and he is good at it, with all the social difficulty such a quality brings with it. The movie costarred Charles Drake, with whom Murphy had worked before and with whom he got along with well. (Drake had played Lattie Tipton's part, "Brandon," in *To Hell and Back*.) Drake's character is a doctor named Luke Canfield who comes to know Gant better than anyone else in town but is still baffled by him. The two play chess together in a central symbolic element of the film and Canfield repeatedly professes his disbelief that Gant could be a cold-blooded killer, simply because he does not look or act like what he thinks a killer should be.

This in fact was the same reaction that many people had when they met Audie Murphy for the first time. How could this boyish face they had seen in magazines be the face of a killer? How could someone who looked so wholesome to the outside world be so psychologically damaged? How much of what a man really is can be visible on the outside? When people got to know Audie Murphy, when they saw his eyes narrow with anger and his face grow cold with determination, they got a fleeting glimpse of what he was like inside and would know the answer to those questions.

In one scene Gant sits at a table in the saloon, sipping coffee (never alcohol) and watches the psychological anguish his reputation is inflicting on the town. Sheriffs and storekeepers literally fall to pieces before his implacable gaze. "Why didn't you kill me?" pleads the sheriff after Gant shoots his gun from his hand. "I wasn't paid to," he answers, just as a man with no patience for pretense or pretending would naturally answer. "Audie Murphy played a very good Audie Murphy," the director later commented. Costar R. G. Armstrong, who played Luke Canfield's father, noted that all good actors have an inner reality, and in *No Name on the Bullet* Murphy seemed to draw deeply on his.[5]

As usual, Murphy spent his free time on the set with only a few people, mostly members of the crew and the stuntmen. One actor, costar John Alderson, spoke with Murphy often, but all they ever talked about was betting on horses, the challenges of raising them, and of dealing with trainers and jockeys. Audie Murphy, he later said, was "as closed as an oyster." His fans, however, who saw him only from the outside, continued to feel very close to him. During the filming, a man from Joplin, Missouri, sent him a pair of chaps he claimed had been worn by Jesse James, and, since Murphy had played the infamous gunslinger long ago in *The Kid From Texas*, maybe he would like to wear them in *No Name on the Bullet*.[6]

That fall, Murphy filmed two more movies, neither of which bore much distinction, and in the middle of December the gossip columns were abuzz with rumors that he had moved out of his house and was now living at the Hollywood Landmark Motor Hotel, a block off Hollywood Boulevard. He had just wrapped up shooting *Cast a Long Shadow* and was disappointed at how the film turned out, although his acting in it was sound. Terry Moore, his female costar, said that throughout the filming Murphy had a particularly bad attitude. He hated the script; he hated the director, and constantly griped that everything was "terrible." Another costar, Wright King, who had not known him previously, came away from the project not liking Murphy at all. Murphy was seemingly morose, kept to himself, and when he emerged he was "kind of a grouch," King said. The movie looked as though it had been filmed on the cheap. It was shot in black and white, his first western to be so filmed, and used recycled footage from other westerns like a cattle stampede from director Howard Hawks's 1948 classic *Red River.* Murphy was so upset with the final product that he dissolved the partnership he had formed with producer Walter M. Mirisch to make the film. Subsequent film historians have generally agreed with Murphy's assessment of the movie. Bob Larkins and Boyd Magers write sadly that *Cast a Long Shadow* was the film that "clearly marked the beginning of Murphy's decline as an important personality in the eyes of Hollywood and the public." The film's faults came from its weak script, heavy-handed music, and low budget, not from Audie Murphy's acting. Nevertheless, it did mark a downward turn in his career.[7]

Meanwhile, Murphy's marriage was coming apart as well. Director Budd Boetticher, who had first worked with Murphy in 1952 on *The Cimarron Kid* and had since become friends with him, said that despite the appearance that they gave to many of only occasionally disrupted marital bliss, in reality Murphy and his wife were "like oil and water." Pamela was an avid churchgoer, and he refused to accompany her, sometimes referring to her to friends as "the reverend." She knew about at least some of his affairs, stoically enduring his infidelity. Though Murphy loved his children, he and his wife separated several times, with Murphy, perhaps unwittingly, replicating the pattern of absences his own father had inflicted on his family long before.[8]

In the late 1950s the movie business was changing. The breath-taking success of television was creating a very unsettled environment among studios, directors, and film actors as it encroached more and more on the entertainment monopoly the movies had long enjoyed. Only the biggest names in directing and acting knew their careers were secure. As studios began diversifying into the television business, they wanted their contract actors and actresses to make television shows as well as movies. At first, Murphy resisted going into television, but in November 1957, he made his first big television appearance, starring in an early episode of NBC's dramatic mystery series *Suspicion*. Murphy played a pilot hired to carry a kidnapped professor to South America. In reality, Murphy was a skilled, licensed pilot himself, and owned an airplane, which he used mostly to travel to and from his ranch in Arizona. He also built a runway on his smaller ranch in Riverside County. When he was filming on locations that were further away from Los Angeles, like Lone Pine, California, or when he worked on *The Unforgiven* with John Huston in Mexico, he often flew himself to the sets. In February 1958, Murphy was on television again, starring as a Confederate soldier in a forgettable thirty-minute episode of *G. E. Theatre*.

His most substantive television project began in 1959 when he signed on to star in *Whispering Smith*, a series in which he played a detective named Tom Smith in 1870s-era Denver. The cast included Guy Mitchell as Murphy's sidekick and featured a rotating cast of guest stars in each episode. Murphy joked to *TV Guide* that the show was like "*Dragnet* on horseback," but despite his lighthearted attitude in the papers, the studio's determination to keep costs down (they budgeted for just $45,000 an episode) concerned him, and the production was plagued with myriad difficulties. His contract pledged him to do a whopping eighty-six episodes of the program and they had filmed only seven of the half-hour episodes when Mitchell fell from a horse and broke his shoulder. Filming came to a stop for six weeks, and by the time Mitchell recovered, Murphy had gone off for a month to shoot a routine western called *Hell Bent for Leather.* The following May, actor Sam Buffington, another regular on the show, whose previous credits included numerous episodes of western TV staples *Maverick, Laramie, Gunsmoke,* and *Wanted: Dead or Alive,* committed suicide at age twenty-eight. Murphy, who by now was growing more outspoken with his frustrations about the show and starting to lose interest in the entire project, made a comment in poor taste to a Los Angeles newspaper about Buffington's suicide, bringing himself and the show more criticism. A new producer, and then yet another, were brought in to reenergize the series, before it was disrupted by a writers' strike. In all, only twenty-six episodes of *Whispering Smith* were completed, and they did not air until 1961. When the show was finally cancelled Murphy said it was the best news he had heard in years.

*Whispering Smith* soured Audie Murphy on television. His final foray into television work came in 1960 with an episode of *Ford Startime.* Unlike the programs with which he had previously been involved, *Startime* was broadcast live from New York City, and so was similar to acting in live theater, something Murphy had not done since his 1947 performance in the play about housing for returning war veterans. His *Startime* episode was entitled "The Man," and was based on a 1950 Broadway play that had won its lead actor, Don Hamner, a Theater World Award. Murphy flew to New York City where he and the cast rehearsed for six days, during which time he impressed his costars with his professionalism but, as usual, was far more reserved and withdrawn than the other actors were accustomed to. The original script was trimmed to under an hour, and Murphy's portrayal of a psychotic who terrorizes actress Thelma Ritter certainly won no awards. One TV critic panned the episode as being "flat and thin," far below the show's usual quality, with Murphy himself never able to seem "menacing or calculating."[9]

The critics might not like him, but that did not mean he lacked star power. In fact, after he returned to California, Murphy was present for the unveiling of his star on the famous Hollywood Walk of Fame, near the corner of Vine Street and Selma Avenue.

---

During the time he worked on *Whispering Smith*, Audie Murphy also appeared on NBC's variety program, *The Dinah Shore Chevy Show*. Roy Rogers and Dale Evans co-hosted the show and provided much of the music each week. Atop hay bales, Murphy sang a song with Rogers and fellow guest, Eddy Arnold. Murphy was a longtime fan of country-western music. Nashville guitarist Chet Atkins was one of his favorite performers and his fellow Texan Bob Wills's hit "San Antonio Rose" was his favorite song.

The enjoyable experience of singing with Rogers and Arnold did not convince Murphy to abandon Hollywood for a career in Nashville, but it did coincide with his becoming friends with Guy Mitchell, his *Whispering Smith* costar. Mitchell was himself a country-western singer and songwriter, whose recording of the classic "Heartaches by the Number" spent two weeks at the top of *Billboard* magazine's Hot 100 singles chart in December 1959. He introduced Murphy to another songwriter named Scotty Turner, a Canadian who had played and written songs with Buddy Holly and then, after coming to California, joined up with Mitchell's band.

Audie Murphy had dabbled in writing poetry before, and now discovered he had something of a gift for turning a good lyrical phrase in his favorite musical style. He and Turner, who was a natural collaborator when it came to songwriting, wound up writing several country-western songs together. His lyrics were often melancholy and reflective, and sometimes intensely personal. Their first was "Shutters and Boards" which they wrote one evening in 1962 when Turner was visiting Murphy at his California ranch. It's not hard to see something of a confession within his words: "The house that we've built was once filled with laughter / But I changed that laughter to tears. Now I live in a world without sunshine / Oh, I wish you were here." The song became a hit for several big name recording artists like Dean Martin, Porter Waggoner, and Jimmy Dean.

Their second song began to take shape when Murphy remarked that the wind blowing around his house always made him feel lonely. The resulting song was "When the Wind Blows in Chicago," and was a hit for Bobby Bare, Roy Clark, and Eddy Arnold. By 1970, when Murphy wrote the equally pensive lyrics for Charlie Pride's hit "Was It All Worth Losing You," he had written almost twenty songs.

———————

In April 1960, Audie Murphy starred in the second and final film he made with director John Huston, United Artists' *The Unforgiven*. As had been the case in *Night Passage*, in *The Unforgiven* he was not the main star and his performance was notably strong, perhaps in part because he did not feel the burden of carrying the movie by himself. Murphy was part of an impressive cast that featured Burt Lancaster as his older brother, Audrey Hepburn as his adopted sister, and Lillian Gish, a star of the silent era, as his mother. As was the case with *The Red Badge of Courage*, Huston's budget was large—at $5.5

million this was the most expensive movie Murphy ever made. He once again responded warmly to how Huston handled him as an actor and did some of his most raw and emotional work. He broke down in tears for one scene, acted wildly drunk in another, and berserk with rage in another. He also grew a mustache for the part which greatly changed the look of his face. His bitter, angry character, Cash Zachary, was the first completely unsympathetic role Murphy had ever played.

One of his costars found him unsympathetic in real life as well. Lillian Gish openly disliked Murphy, complaining that he was a trigger-happy lunatic who would shoot at anything or anyone. She even flatly refused to ride in a car with him. With his penchant for practical jokes like tossing a sack of snakes into a room full of unsuspecting people or showing off his shooting skills, he was definitely not her type.

Though Huston drew a good performance out of Murphy, and though *The Unforgiven* was a critical success, it was a commercial failure. So for Murphy it was back to making inexpensive B-movie westerns. His next movie was an unremarkable film titled *Posse from Hell*, a project that was notable only because it reunited him with actor Royal Dano from *The Red Badge of Courage*.

Murphy's next movie was a war film. Luridly titled *Battle at Bloody Beach*, it was set in the Philippines during World War II. The melodramatic plot had Murphy, cast as a civilian working for the Navy, searching for his missing wife while delivering guns and supplies to Filipino guerillas fighting the Japanese. The film coincided with a perceptible change in tone among some critics in how they looked at war films in general. "True to the traditions of Hollywood," noted the *New York Times* dismissively, Murphy waged the war against the Japanese "not to free the Philippines but to win a blonde."[10]

This was not simply a glib remark by a grumpy film critic, however. A change was underway among national opinion-shapers about war itself: its valor, its cost, its very legitimacy. "Our movies go right on suggesting that warfare is a sort of killing game that large teams of men engage in on suitable occasions and that can even, at times, be fun," the paper complained. In *Battle at Bloody Beach*, Murphy's "one man destruction of a couple of battalions of enemy soldiers...is like a rip-roaring turkey shoot." It said that behind most Hollywood war movies was a "massive naiveté" that was actually dangerous to the country. There was, the paper charged, genuine "peril in prolonging the old illusion that war is for heroes and heroic death. War is for monsters and mad men. Our films should say so."

No one needed to lecture Audie Murphy on the horrors of war. No film critic had seen as much of what war was really like as he had. Murphy understood the human cost of war, among the living as well as the dead, as much as anyone could. He nevertheless adhered to the patriotic attitudes that were quickly falling out of favor with film critics and filmmakers. As such, he became an even more attractive target for his critics.

An official U.S. Army film that Audie Murphy made in the summer of 1960 embodied his continued authority as spokesman for the military. Entitled *The Big Picture: The Broken Bridge with Audie Murphy*, it was "an official report produced for the armed forces and the American people," and opened with Murphy walking into his living room to find his two sons playing army on the floor. "Who won the battle?" he asks. His son Terry hands him a rocket, asking if he can fix it. "I don't know anything about missiles, Ter," he answers. Off he then goes to Europe on a trip "to find out about these new weapons." In making this movie he returned to Germany for the first time since 1945. He walks the vast, empty stadium at Nuremburg where the Nazi rallies had taken place and where at the end of years of fighting he had seen the American flag raised. In a voiceover he explains that Hitler was only stopped by the determination and sacrifice of men like his fallen buddies. "Their blood feeds the weeds that you see growing now—men who wanted to live just as much as you and I." Now, in the wake of their sacrifice, "the price of peace is eternal vigilance."

In the film, Murphy, always dressed in coat and tie, travels as far north as Oslo, as far south as Venice, and to border of the East Germany, meeting with American troops and America's NATO partners. The alert viewer might note that American officers salute him, a civilian—a distinction reserved for presidents and winners of the Medal of Honor. Throughout the movie, Murphy appears earnest and engaged—more so than in many of his dramatic films. In one scene, a colonel goes over a map, pencil in his hand, and remarks to Murphy, "I never thought I'd be telling you anything about combat." The cold, stern look that flashes for a moment in Murphy's eyes is a little chilling. The Army newspaper *Stars and Stripes* noted that Murphy refused to talk about his wartime experiences while making the film, and usually tried to dismiss any inquiries with a joke or by changing the subject. He also guarded his reputation as an authentic tough guy. When a crew member came up during a break and told him to have a seat so he could reapply Murphy's face powder for the cameras, he refused: "Oh no, you don't. You're not going to set me down and put on makeup in front of the whole damn army."[11]

At the end of the film, back in his living room with Terry and Skipper, Murphy addresses the viewer and says "today's Army is one we can all be mighty proud of," and because of its strength, "you and I can be more secure." It was what he had been saying to audiences since his very first speech on a hot summer day in Farmersville just a week after coming home from the war. For his work in the film, which played in both military and civilian theaters, the Army gave Audie Murphy its Outstanding Civilian Service Award.

---

Film audiences had not grown tired of Audie Murphy or of films about World War II. In 1961, 20th Century Fox announced it was making an epic movie about D-Day, *The Longest Day*, and Universal announced that it was going to re-release *To Hell and Back*. At the end of 1962 he appeared in San Antonio at the premiere of *The Longest Day* and took part in a memorial service at Fort Sam Houston to honor those who died on the Normandy beaches.[12]

But there was also a crescendo of voices worried about violence on television and in motion pictures. In the summer of 1961 Congress took up an investigation into whether violent movies and particularly violence on television were contributing to juvenile delinquency. As an example of violence on television, the Senate subcommittee on Juvenile Delinquency showed the second episode of *Whispering Smith*. "Those brutal sadistic films and shows on television are outrageous," said Senator Thomas Dodd of Connecticut. "I've never heard anyone say these violent programs are anything but awful." Senator John Carroll of Colorado called Murphy's show a libel on his hometown of Denver and said that it was bad for adults as well as children.[13]

While the culture was shifting under his feet in subtle but substantive ways, Murphy's sense of morality remained the same. He disdained making commercials that advertised tobacco or alcohol because he wanted to set a good example for young people, but he had no problem making westerns. "They're a good escape from everyday life," he said, and give the audience "color and scenery that they can't get on TV." For the next few years he made a string of low-budget westerns even as the genre itself was disappearing. The other

B-movie western stars from the 1950s like Randolph Scott, Gene Autry, Roy Rogers, and Johnny Mack Brown were retiring. But not him. "I seem to be the only one left," he said, but "I'll keep on making them until they get wise to me." The faces, the plots, the action, the dialogue stayed the same, he said with his modest smile. "Only the horses get changed."[14]

In quick succession came forgettable movies with exciting titles like 6 Black Horses, Showdown, Gunfight at Comanche Creek, The Quick Gun, and Bullet for a Bad Man. They were easy. The dialogue was simple. "Audie learned his craft within his own limitations," said actor Jan Merlin. Murphy himself had reputedly acknowledged that limitation years earlier on the set of his first starring role. "You forget that I've got a hell of a handicap," he told Bad Boy director Kurt Neumann when he was coaching Murphy on some point of acting. "What handicap?" Neumann asked. "No talent," Murphy grinned.

In 1963, Murphy provided the narration and an introduction to a low budget movie by Allied Artists about the Korean War entitled War Is Hell. In every war, he says, speaking from the depths of experience, there is combat between soldier and soldier, but also "there's the personal war, sometimes even more deadly, that each man has inside himself." War pushes young men "to the limit of man's physical and mental endurance." In referring to one of the movie's characters who breaks under the strain, he says, "War uprooted and revealed the rotten core of the man. Combat does this."

"The point is, I think, that a man will not be strong enough to face any really critical situation unless he has the right equipment, and the most modern weapons are not enough. He must be armed with moral strength as well."

The sleeping pills on which Audie Murphy was growing more reliant were a poor substitute for moral strength, the guns he enjoyed shooting provided no lasting sense of security, and his money trouble, which was growing ever more dire from gambling, was driving him to a tragic end.

# CHAPTER TWELVE

# NO NAME ON THE BULLET

I n the mid-1960s Audie Murphy seemed increasingly out of touch with the leftward drift of American popular culture. His heroism in World War II, and the public celebration of that heroism, now looked more antiquated than praiseworthy. But even if the culture was changing, Murphy was not. He had no sympathy with the anti–Vietnam War movement and the draft protests, and his response was to continue to trumpet the virtues of military service. "There is a growing tendency to regard military service as an onerous chore rather than an exciting opportunity," he said late in the decade. "The chance to serve one's country is a high privilege, not a wearisome sacrifice." He exhorted Americans not to "downgrade the noble profession which guarantees our freedom."[1]

Though he disapproved of the leftward turn of the Democratic Party, he supported its candidates through the 1968 presidential campaign, where he endorsed Hubert Humphrey over Richard Nixon.

There was also a trend in the film industry to turn away from the sort of films that had shaped Audie Murphy as a young man, films like *Sergeant York*. As Murphy commented in 1962, "It's out of mode nowadays to be patriotic. If you show patriotism you can be considered a subversive."[2]

There were still popular western series on television and a few westerns in the movies, but there was no mistaking that the more trendy Hollywood producers were turning against them, especially the sort of predictable, traditional, conservative, low-budget westerns, with lots of action and simple morality that had made up the bulk of Audie Murphy's career. "Pass some pot around the screen and you've got a line around the block," said producer Norman Jewison of the current trends in movies. "Political radicalism finds a marketplace as surely as our war films once did." Exit Audie Murphy, *Variety* quipped, enter Peter Fonda. But Audie Murphy was not ready to exit.[3]

Like many actors, Murphy feared how getting older "shows up on the screen. Age is the worst thing of all. Time is what's chasing you." But Murphy could still command a big enough audience to earn a paycheck making the sort of movies he knew how to make.[4]

In June 1965, Murphy completed work on *Gunpoint*, his last movie with Gordon Kay, the producer behind many of his westerns in the early 1960s. "I don't think Audie was an actor," said his *Gunpoint* costar Joan Staley, a former *Playboy* centerfold in 1958 who became an actress, working mostly in television. He was, she said, a "screen persona who acquitted himself well." He did not want to be a star, she thought, as much as he simply wanted to be liked; though that assessment seems off-target. The fact that most people found Murphy charming, self-effacing, and likeable does not imply that he had any great desire to be liked. Audie Murphy was proudly his own man.[5]

Staley got closer to understanding him when she said, "I don't want to say he was an unhappy man, but a man at odds with his situation." That observation mirrors that something that Murphy himself said: "I'm not an actor. I don't even like actors. By that I mean I have nothing in common with them."[6]

Murphy was "a regular guy thrust into an area of earning his livelihood because of an incident of extreme bravery," Staley concluded and she wondered if he might not have been happier doing something else. Murphy sometimes wondered the same thing. Looking back over his career, he thought that he might have made a better stuntman than a leading man.[7]

Staley had never worked with Murphy before, but his other costars in the film who knew him better still saw the man they were familiar with. Denver Pyle remembered that while Murphy kept to himself, as usual, this time around he also had a girlfriend who visited him on the set and liked to ride horses. He still played practical jokes that were sometimes rough, like waving scorpions at people, still spent most of his free time with the crew and stuntmen, and still slept with a .45 pistol at his bedside.

*Gunpoint* was Murphy's last movie with Universal. With its completion his contract came to an end and the studio chose not to renew it. For the first time in fifteen years he was on his own professionally. In quick succession, Murphy went abroad to film two movies, largely because of the lower production costs overseas. The first was an ill-suited spy movie shot in Israel entitled *Trunk to Cairo*, in which Murphy played an American secret agent trying to destroy nuclear missiles based in Egypt. It was a cheaply produced film that tried to cash in on the popularity of the James Bond genre. He in fact called it the worst James Bond parody he had ever read and threatened to back out of the project entirely, even though he had signed a contract. American critics said that the film would add very little to the reputation of Israeli producer Menahem Golan, who went on to produce a string of uneven action movies. Whatever *Trunk to Cairo* may have gained through its internationally known cast—it also starred Academy Award–winning British actor George Sanders—"it loses in its stereotyped script and wooden directing." Only in the action scenes did Murphy look engaged at all.[8]

In 1964 a young actor named Clint Eastwood had starred in *A Fistful of Dollars*, an exceptionally violent and unromanticized—even cynical—reimagining of the traditional western that had been shot in Spain and proved enormously successful. People spoke of it as reinvigorating the genre and it sparked an avalanche of mostly cheaply made "spaghetti westerns": European-made westerns mostly from Italian studios, often filmed in Spain.

In 1965 Murphy went to Spain to film his own Euro-western, *The Texican*. It was another very low-budget film and this time Murphy even had to do all his own stunts because there wasn't enough money to hire a stuntman. He had to do everything but pack his own lunch, he joked. The movie was "a straight-up traditional oater," with none of the violence, cynicism, or moral ambiguity that marked *A Fistful of Dollars*. "By the time *The Texican* reached the screen," wrote one critic, "the rules of the Western were in the midst of being rewritten." It further pushed Murphy to the sidelines of the movie business.[9]

While he was shooting in Spain in the fall of 1965, Murphy was so strung out on the prescription sleeping pill Placidyl that his costars who did not know him thought he was constantly drunk. "I was half asleep all the time," he later admitted, "day and night." His insomnia had grown worse and he turned to stronger medicine to contend with it.[10]

In 1966, he faced the fact that he was addicted. "I was a zombie. I dissipated all my money. I gave it away. I was not interested in anything." He would handle the problem himself, in his own way. "I knew what I had to do," he said. He checked into a hotel in Florida, threw away his pills, and locked himself in his room for five days. It was a rough withdrawal; he felt "just like a junkie." But he got through it. "I won't take another pill," he said a year later. "Not one." At home, he converted the garage in his house to a bedroom where he started sleeping nights, or at least trying to. He would sleep with the lights on so that whenever he woke up from a combat dream he would know immediately where he was. He still carried a gun "for protection and therapy." One of his biographers writes that during these tough years Murphy "was leading a life that drifted further and further away from the safe moorings of marriage and home." Nothing represented that quite as vividly as the effects his gambling was having. By the end of the 1960s, Murphy was placing more racing bets through bookies in other cities, especially Chicago and Miami, instead of in person at southern California racetracks. Doing so obviously gave him many more opportunities for excitement but also brought him in close contact with people and groups that ran off-track betting services, people in whom the FBI also had an interest. He began losing tens of thousands of dollars at a time and had to borrow money from several banks to keep up with his debts. In the fall of 1969 alone he lost more than $90,000. On those occasions when he won, however, he found it nearly impossible to collect. He began taping his phone conversations.[11]

Because of his notoriety as a gambler with connections to bookmaking operations and numerous racetracks, the FBI recruited him to work under cover, providing them with information on mobsters with whom he might come into contact.[12]

If that was an acting job in the service of law enforcement, he tried to continue his career acting before the motion picture cameras as well. In his last few movies Audie Murphy's youthful face finally gave way to one more compatible with the parts he was playing. He did not suddenly appear old like he thought, but his face gained some lines and with them some character. It helped him on camera, allowing for his serious style of delivery to be much more convincing. One of the drawbacks in many of his early movies had been that his extremely youthful face was often incompatible with the grim determination that so often characterized his performances. It was not a sign of poor acting, but it gave no impression so much as one of a child pretending. It was, therefore, hard for some critics to take him seriously.

In 1967's *40 Guns to Apache Pass,* the last film in which he played a starring role, he gave a good performance that was nevertheless wasted in an otherwise mediocre movie. In it, there is a poignant exchange between Murphy's cavalry captain and a wounded sergeant, played by Robert Brubaker, whom he is trying to protect from Apaches after pulling him into a small cleft in a rocky cliff. Grimacing from his wound, the sergeant looks at the captain and says, "You got more guts than any man I ever knew. Must've been bred in you." After a pause Murphy replies, "Not exactly. Actually I come from a long line of losers, Sergeant. Matter of fact, my family motto was 'if at first you don't succeed give up.'" After another grimace, the sergeant says, "You sure switched that around somewhere." "I tried to," he answers.

As Murphy's film career was coming to an end, one sympathetic reporter wrote that as an actor Murphy had simply been played out, and "exploited by half the hack producers in Hollywood." They put him in the kinds of movies that turned a profit as long as the expenses were kept low. Though Murphy had always professed to like making westerns, he now recognized that he had been typecast into irrelevance. "You make a success in westerns," he said, and "they milk it dry— until you're dry."[13] But he was determined not to give up, not to be someone who just turned tail and ran. "I'm too tough for this damn town," he said defiantly of Hollywood. "It can't break my heart."[14]

In February 1968, Murphy returned to Hunt County to attend the funeral of his younger brother Joe, a policeman who had been killed in a car wreck. At the funeral he was reunited with his estranged father. Audie put his arm around Emmett Murphy, leaned in close, and talked to his father for the first time in decades.

Later that year, Murphy formed a production company to raise money for a series of movies with director Budd Boetticher. He had first worked with Boetticher in 1951 on *The Cimarron Kid* and considered him a friend. Later in the 1950s the director made a series of successful low-budget westerns with Randolph Scott. Now their goal was to make old-fashioned entertaining movies that shied away from the social commentary that was become so prevalent in films. Murphy would occasionally play a few secondary roles, but his primary job would be not acting, but producing. He wanted to use young actors "with some good old pros to back them up." Some of the money came from the Clinton Oil Company in Wichita, Kansas, (then one of the largest independent oil companies in the country). Its president Rick Clinton was also a vice president for Murphy's company, which was called First Investment Planning Company, or FIPCO. "I didn't care for Audie's associates," Boetticher later said of the money men, "but I didn't have to spend any time with them."[15]

Murphy's final performance on camera came in a five-minute cameo in the movie *A Time for Dying*. In it, Murphy, sporting a beard, played an older Jesse James who gives the film's main character tips on being a gunfighter. Murphy played his part well. "He was excellent," said Boetticher, "even if he didn't think much of himself as an actor." The movie was shot in Apache Junction, outside of Phoenix. Both of Murphy's sons had small parts in the film. Murphy and Boetticher previewed the completed movie in Dallas, as a benefit for the American Kidney Foundation, but it would not have a wider release until over ten years later.[16]

Murphy and Boetticher had two more projects already on the drawing board—one, *A Horse for Mr. Barnum*, they intended to shoot in Spain, and the other, *When There's Sumpthin' To Do*, was to be filmed in northeast Mexico, with production beginning in October 1969. This time Murphy was going to star in the picture, something that might help it commercially, and both men seemed excited about the prospects of reinvigorating the market for good old-fashioned "oaters." Terry Murphy, now seventeen, was going to costar with his father, along with a well-known Mexican bullfighter named Gaston Santos.[17]

All else, however, seemed to be falling apart. Murphy had recently lost almost $300,000 in an oil deal in Algeria; the IRS was garnishing his earnings from television reruns of his movies because he owed $250,000 in back taxes; and he found it impossible to save any money. "He was generous to everybody who touched him for a loan," a Houston reporter noted, "but never asked for anything from anyone."[18]

The month that filming on the next FIPCO movie was set to begin, Murphy was sued by Bank of America and the National Trust and Savings Association for non-payment of a $15,500 loan he had taken out two years before. They were not alone. There were numerous such lawsuits. Over the course of his movie career Audie Murphy had earned nearly $3 million but by September 1968 he was unable to pay off another $13,000 loan, this one to a bank in Dallas. By now he had sold a boat, his airplane, and his ranches, and declared bankruptcy in 1968. He told Boetticher, however, that once he got his debts paid off, "I'll be starting all over again."[19]

That was not his only bad news. His temper continued to get him into trouble and cloud his once sterling reputation. In the summer of 1970, he stood trial on assault charges stemming from a messy altercation he had with a dog trainer. A girlfriend of Murphy's named Marie D'Auria was unhappy with the job the trainer had done with her dog, a German Shepherd named Rommel that Murphy had given her, and after overhearing a heated phone call between her and the trainer, Murphy and a friend paid the man a visit. Some sort of fight ensued. At the trial there were conflicting accounts of who hit whom and whether Murphy shot at the trainer with intent to kill. In October, a Burbank jury cleared him of all the charges.[20]

In August, while the trial was still going on, Murphy continued to cut deals, trying to arrange projects that could give a boost to his career as a film producer. That month he acquired the rights to two screenplays, both written by Rodney W. Jones, one entitled "Stand Proud, My Son," the other "Empire of Rodents." Neither came to anything.[21]

———————

In May 1968, Murphy agreed to host a radio show called "Beyond the Call." Each program would be four and a half minutes long, recalling the exploits of a Medal of Honor winner. The series of 260 programs was produced by Murray Woroner, himself a veteran of World War II in the Pacific. It was a great idea and Murphy's calm voice, with its slight Texan drawl, came across well on radio.[22] In June, he gave the dedication address for a War Memorial in Decatur, Alabama. By now the war in Vietnam was dominating the headlines and Murphy thought about it often. It had become a "no-win war," he told a Montgomery newspaper, "a war of frustration. We have lost sight of the objective," which was that "we're there to fight communism." Of the protesters against the war, he said, "I'd hate their guts if they had any."[23]

Because of his military fame and his outspoken nature, in 1971 Murphy found himself wrapped up in the national debate over the conviction of a first lieutenant in the Army named William L. Calley Jr. who was accused of killing civilians in Vietnam in an affair that came to be known as the My Lai Massacre. Few understood the incredible pressures that occur on a man during combat better than Murphy. "I'm not so sure that in those days," he said, speaking of WWII, "having been indoctrinated to a fever pitch, I might not have committed the same error, and I prefer to call it an error—that Lieutenant Calley did."[24]

In the middle of all the negative press the Army was then receiving, Audie Murphy saw the movie *Patton* which 20th Century Fox released to great fanfare in April 1971. He was very impressed with all parts of the film and in May he telephoned the film's producer Frank McCarthy to compliment him on his work. Divulging no details as of yet, Murphy vaguely explained that he had a "terrific project" in mind that he wanted to discuss with McCarthy. McCarthy said he was interested and proposed that the two speak again as soon as Murphy returned from a business trip he had scheduled.[25]

Shortly after their conversation, Murphy flew to Atlanta to check out another business deal that he hoped could help him recover from his Algerian oil debacle. A company called Modular Properties that built prefabricated buildings wanted to use him to attract potential investors.

After meeting with its executives in Atlanta, he and four others from the company flew in a small chartered plane to Martinsville, Virginia, where the company had a plant so that Murphy could see for himself how the company constructed its buildings.

Sixty miles outside of Martinsville the weather turned cloudy and rainy, and lowering fog kept them from landing. The pilot contacted the airport in Roanoke, Virginia, about forty miles to the north, and was told that conditions there were not yet bad enough to close the runway. So instead of diverting southward toward Greensboro, almost equidistant in the opposite direction, the pilot turned the plane toward Roanoke. The problem with turning north was that it took the plane into more mountainous and heavily wooded country, terrain with which the pilot had very little experience. Some time after 11:00 in the morning, the pilot contacted Roanoke's Woodrum Field and was told that the ceiling there was 1,000 feet and visibility was three miles, safe for visual flight rules. He radioed back that he intended to land.

That was the last transmission from the aircraft. The small plane slammed into the western side of Brushy Mountain in the Jefferson National Forest, twelve miles northwest of Roanoke. It disintegrated on impact 300 feet below the mountain's 3,000 foot summit where visibility was near zero. Everyone on board was killed. After the plane was reported missing, it took a full three days for crews searching from civilian air patrols to find the wreckage in the thick forest, which they finally did early on the afternoon of Monday, May 31— Memorial Day. Even then it required an aerial spotter in a helicopter to direct people on the ground up to the remote crash site. A lieutenant with the state police reported that the bodies were "badly mangled" and those in the wreckage had burned. Murphy had been thrown clear of the plane. The coroner's office identified him by the nine-inch scar from the German sniper's bullet that sent him to the hospital in 1944. He was a month shy of his forty-sixth birthday.[26]

An honor guard comprised of local reserve officers met Audie Murphy's flag-draped casket at the Roanoke airport and saw it loaded aboard a flight to the west coast. His body was returned to Los Angeles for a memorial service on June 4, 1971, that was attended by hundreds of people. Stuntmen, film technicians, and crew hands filled the pews of the Church of the Hills in Forest Lawn Memorial Park. The only stars who attended were Wanda Hendrix and Ann Blyth, who had come to know Murphy during junket trips for *The Kid from Texas*. Hendrix, now twice divorced herself, wept quietly as she touched the casket. There were six Medal of Honor winners who came to honor one of their own. An Army Chaplain from a nearby post delivering the eulogy called Murphy one of the Army's "most courageous warriors," and as a civilian, "a quiet unassuming man." Terry Hunt, in whose gym Murphy had once bunked when he was down on his luck, served as one of the pallbearers.[27]

That same day, friends and family from Hunt County gathered for a memorial service at the First Baptist Church in Farmersville, where Murphy's mother's funeral had been held in 1941. Businesses in the small town closed between two and three that afternoon. Flags around Texas were flown at half-staff for three days.

After the service in Los Angeles, Murphy's body was flown to Arlington National Cemetery, where full honors awaited him. Among those in attendance for the ceremony in the chapel at Fort Myer were almost forty World War II veterans from Murphy's 3rd Infantry Division, including Major Kenneth Potter, one of his commanding officers in France and the man who had written the citation for his Medal of Honor. "I never knew a better soldier," Potter said simply. Terry Hunt came east with Pamela Murphy and the boys to serve once again as a pallbearer for his old friend. Theater executive James Cherry came up from Dallas. Also there paying their respects were General William Westmoreland, the Chief of Staff of the Army, and George H. W. Bush, the American Ambassador to the United Nations. President Richard Nixon sent his military aide, Lieutenant Colonel Vernon Coffee, to represent the White House. The Army Band from Fort Myer led the procession and Murphy's casket was carried on a caisson pulled by six black horses to his gravesite near the Tomb of the Unknowns. Hundreds of mourners watched in silence as Audie Murphy was lowered into the ground in a simple walnut casket. Buried just to his right was a soldier who had been killed in Vietnam the previous summer. The United States said goodbye to its most decorated soldier from World War II. A column in the *Dallas Morning*

*News* marking his passing noted somberly that "Audie Murphy came from an America that no longer exists, a small town America in which the lines clearly were drawn between right and wrong, good and evil." Although American soldiers would continue to fight in wars, there would be no more quite like him.[28]

---

"How many of you have heard the name Audie Murphy?" I asked two separate history classes in the fall semester of 2014. It was the basic U.S. history survey, not a specialized upper-division class, and the students were all undergraduates, from freshman to seniors. About three in each class of thirty-five said they had. "He was an actor, wasn't he?" one young man ventured. "He fought in World War II," said another, his forehead furrowed in concentration. Most of them seemed to have little notion that Murphy was someone whose name they should know. "I bet your grandparents know him," I told them. "Ask them over Christmas break if you get the chance."

The Pearl Harbor veteran of whom I asked the same question a day later had a quite different response. "He was a magnificent soldier," he said in a strong and gravelly voice, leaning forward in his chair with a sudden burst of energy, his hand shaking slightly on the head of his cane. "Just a magnificent soldier. He was everything a soldier should be. He was a leader," he added after a moment's pause. "Almost every man can be brave if he has to, but not every man can be a real leader and be an example for other men to follow. Audie Murphy was a leader. He was the ideal soldier."

For Americans after World War II, Murphy was more than an ideal soldier—he was a hero, a living embodiment of the virtues of selflessness, perseverance, loyalty, and patriotism. And in some ways he had lived the American Dream, starting out dirt poor and not only serving courageously in battle, but rising into the ranks of Hollywood stardom. But for Audie Murphy, heroism and celebrity were simply incompatible. The brutal reality of combat was real; Hollywood stardom was fake. He made an uneasy peace with Hollywood by disliking actors, denigrating his own acting ability, and spending his time on the sets with the working men on the crew—the stuntmen, the hired hands, the men who did an honest day's work with very little pretending.

Almost without fail, people who met Audie Murphy for the first time and were familiar with his exploits in the war were surprised to find the most decorated soldier in American history to be quiet and withdrawn, to be shy and humble. Murphy felt he had made no conscious choice to be heroic; he had simply done what had to be done, just as all his buddies did. He did not want to talk about it, in part because he had a survivor's guilt over the many other brave soldiers who had not beaten the law of averages, as he had, and who had paid the ultimate price.

In the impressive combat record of the men of Murphy's regiment is written the grim fact that it was on the front lines for so long, engaged with the enemy for months on end. In his Company B, almost all the men who started out with him were gone by the end of the war. To Murphy, survival could seem less a matter of heroic effort and more a matter of chance. In what way could that be worthy of celebration? As he said many times, the real heroes were dead.

In August 1955, a newspaper columnist noted that "every school boy able to utter the syllables can identify Audie Murphy as 'the most decorated GI of World War II.'" Sixty years on from that, and seventy after the end of the war, the children and grandchildren of those school boys now have no idea who he was.[29]

Audie Murphy reminds us of the lingering human cost of any war, even one whose end was so triumphant as World War II. Hero that he surely was, movie star that he became, he never emerged from under the shadow of the war that made him famous.

# ACKNOWLEDGMENTS

I 'd like to thank Tom Spence, Harry Crocker, and Lauren Mann at Regnery. I can't imagine a better team of editors with whom to work. Thanks to Susan Lanning and Linda Owens at the Audie Murphy/American Cotton Museum in Greenville, Texas, which is a small but wonderful museum dedicated to preserving the memory of Audie Murphy. The photos included here come from their impressive collection, and for the use of which I offer them special thanks. Any biographer of Audie Murphy will owe a sizeable debt to books like Don Graham's *No Name on the Bullet* and Harold Simpson's *Audie Murphy: American Soldier*, and I'm happy to acknolwedge that debt here.

Many thanks and much appreciation as well to Tom Parrish, a Navy veteran who was at Pearl Harbor on the morning of December 7, 1941, aboard the USS *Vestal*, a support ship moored just outboard of the *Arizona*. He spoke with me at length about Audie Murphy and made it clear just how much WWII veterans, even after the intervening decades, revere Murphy and what he represents.

Thanks as well to Jason Morrow, Robert Collins, James Pohl, and to Kim Kellison, Jeff Hamilton, and my colleagues in the history department at Baylor University, as well as to the staff of the Texas Collection at Baylor.

To my mom and dad, Leo and Barbara Smith, my lifelong thanks and appreciation. To my wife Lorynn, gratitude and appreciation for more than can be enumerated here. And extra thanks to my children, Evan and Charlotte, who have now watched more Audie Murphy movies by far than anyone else in their grades, but were always ready for another one.

David Smith
Waco, Texas
February 2015

# FILMOGRAPHY OF AUDIE MURPHY

## *BEYOND GLORY*
Paramount
Released September 1948
Black and White
Director: John Farrow
Starring: Alan Ladd, Donna Reed, and George Macready

*Beyond Glory* was Audie Murphy's first appearance in a feature film. In it, he played a small part as a West Point cadet and roommate of one of the central characters. He had very little dialogue but director John Farrow commented that "Audie has as much natural acting talent as any newcomer I've ever worked with."

## *TEXAS, BROOKLYN AND HEAVEN*
United Artists
Released July 1948
Black and White
Director: William Castle
Starring: Guy Madison, Diana Lynn, James Dunn

Murphy's second role in a feature film was another small part, this time as a copy boy for a newspaper.

## *BAD BOY*
Allied Artists
Released February 1949
Black and White
Director: Kurt Neumann
Costars: Lloyd Nolan, Jane Wyatt

Audie Murphy's first leading role in a featvure film, in which he plays a juvenile delinquent sent to a boys ranch in central Texas for rehabilitation. The film was co-produced by Variety Clubs International, a charitable organization that worked with young boys.

## *THE KID FROM TEXAS*
Universal-International
Released March 1950
Technicolor
Director: Kurt Neumann
Costars: Gayle Storm, Will Geer, Albert Dekker

Audie Murphy's first western, in which he plays Billy the Kid during the 1879 "Lincoln County War" in New Mexico.

## SIERRA

Universal-International
Released May 1950
Technicolor
Director: Alfred E. Green
Costars: Tony Curtis (billed then usually as "Anthony"),
James Arness, Burl Ives.

Filmed in Utah with impressive scenery, this is the one film in which Murphy stars with his first wife, actress Wanda Hendrix. Murphy stars as a young man who, with his father, breaks wild horses.

## KANSAS RAIDERS

Universal-International
Released November 1950
Technicolor
Director: Ray Enright
Costars: Brian Donlevy, Tony Curtis, Marguerite Chapman,
Richard Long. (*Kansas Raiders* was also Murphy's first film with
fellow B-western stalwart James Best, who would become
his most regular costar.)

In this movie, Audie Murphy plays Jesse James in a fanciful retelling of the story of the James brothers and the Younger brothers riding with the infamous "Quantrill's Raiders" operating in Kansas during the American Civil War. James Best plays Cole Younger; Richard Long plays Frank James.

## THE RED BADGE OF COURAGE
MGM
Released September 1951
Black and White
Director: John Huston
Costars: Bill Mauldin (the WWII cartoonist), Royal Dano,
Douglas Dick, Andy Devine

One of Audie Murphy's best turns as an actor in the film version of Stephen Crane's classic short novel about courage on the battlefield. Murphy very authoritatively portrays a soldier struggling with his fear. The film suffers greatly because of the editing done at the insistence of the studio once John Huston left to film *The African Queen*. This was the first clear indication of how good an actor Murphy could be when given the right director and the right script.

## THE CIMARRON KID
Universal-International
Released January 1952
Color
Director: Budd Boetticher
Costars: Hugh O'Brian, Noah Beery, Jr.,
James Best, Yvette Duguay

Murphy plays a member of the historic Dalton gang known as "The Cimarron Kid" in this western. Notable for little more than a couple of good action sequences, the film represents a disappointing step back from the progress he had shown in *The Red Badge of Courage.*

## THE DUEL AT SILVER CREEK

Universal-International
Released August 1952
Technicolor
Director: Don Siegel
Costars: Stephen McNally, Will Geer, Faith Domergue, and
Lee Marvin in his first credited movie role

Audie Murphy's character chases down a gang of claim jumpers, after they murder his father. Familiar ground for anyone familiar with western B movies, or for that matter Lone Ranger episodes. Nevertheless there are effective elements including lots of chases and lots of action. There's significantly less character development, however. In a remark that will remind viewers of Murphy's own life story, the town marshal, played by Stephen McNally, says of Murphy's character "He didn't have the face of a killer, but he had the cold steel look of one."

## GUNSMOKE

Universal-International
Released March 1953
Technicolor
Director: Nathan Juran
Costars: Susan Cabot, Paul Kelly. Also the first movie Murphy
made with actors Charles Drake (who would play the part of
Murphy's friend Lattie Tipton in *To Hell and Back*), and Denver
Pyle, who appears here in an uncredited role.

Murphy's first movie with director Nathan Juran with whom he made a series of respectable and effective westerns. Here Murphy plays a gunfighter who winds up owning a ranch who then has to oversee a trail drive to keep it. One of the more highly regarded of Murphy's westerns in the early to mid-1950s.

## COLUMN SOUTH
Universal-International
Released June 1953
Technicolor
Director: Fred deCordova
Costars: Joan Evans, Robert Sterling, Dennis Weaver,
James Best, Denver Pyle, and Russell Johnson (who like Murphy
was a decorated veteran of WWII, having been shot
down over the Philippines)

Audie Murphy plays a cavalry officer on the New Mexico frontier right before the Civil War who heads off an Indian uprising engineered by Confederate agents. Director Fred deCordova later claimed that he had to change the camera angle for one of the close-ups of Murphy's character because the anger in his eyes would have scared the audience.

## TUMBLEWEED
Universal-International
Released December 1953
Technicolor
Director: Nathan Juran
Costars: Chill Wills, Lee Van Cleef, Lori Nelson, Russell Johnson

Audie Murphy's character guards a wagon train as it proceeds westward and is arrested when it is attacked by Indians. He then has to work to prove he wasn't somehow involved in setting up the attack. Part of the movie was filmed in Death Valley, California.

## RIDE CLEAR OF DIABLO
Universal-International
Released March 1954
Technicolor
Director: Jesse Hibbs
Costars: Susan Cabot, Dan Duryea, Jack Elam (who became one of Murphy's closer friends in the business and long-time gambling buddy), Denver Pyle, Russell Johnson

Murphy plays a railroad surveyor chasing cattle rustlers who killed his father.

## DRUMS ACROSS THE RIVER
Universal-International
Released June 1954
Technicolor
Director: Nathan Juran
Costars: Jay Silverheels (who, since 1949 had been playing Tonto in the television Lone Ranger), Walter Brennan (one of the most famous character actors in Hollywood westerns), Hugh O'Brian, Lyle Bettger

A very solid western in which Murphy plays a character trying to protect his father while heading off an Indian war engineered by miners who want to hunt for gold on Ute Indian land.

## DESTRY
Universal-International
Released November 1954
Technicolor
Director: George Marshall
Costars: Lyle Bettger, Lori Nelson, Alan Hale, Jr.

A close remake of 1939's *Destry Rides Again*, which had starred Jimmy Stewart and Marlene Dietrich and which Marshall also directed. A new deputy in a lawless town seeks to bring law and order, despite his youthful appearance.

## TO HELL AND BACK
Universal-International
Released October 1955
Technicolor
Director: Jesse Hibbs
Costars: Marshall Thompson (who some thought should play Audie Murphy in the movie itself), Charles Drake, Denver Pyle, Jack Kelly, David Janssen, Susan Kohner. (Terry Murphy, Audie's older son, plays one of Audie's little brothers in one of the early scenes of life in Hunt County.)

Audie Murphy stars as himself in this film version of his combat memoir. It quickly takes him from a boy in Hunt County to enlistment in the army to the heat of battle, ending with his being awarded the Medal of Honor. Filmed primarily in Washington state, with Fort Lewis and the Yakima River region standing in for Sicily, Italy and France. (MGM had also filmed parts of the WWII movie *Battleground* at Ft. Lewis in 1949.)

## WORLD IN MY CORNER
Universal-International
Released March 1956
Black and White
Director: Jesse Hibbs
Costars: Barbara Rush, Jeff Morrow, John McIntire

Audie Murphy's turn as a boxer was coolly received by a public which expected to see him in settings other than this one. Murphy trained with real boxers and wasn't afraid to take a punch, said his sparring partners. He filmed some of the scenes in New York and New Jersey while he was doing publicity for *To Hell and Back*.

## WALK THE PROUD LAND
Universal-International
Released September 1956
Technicolor
Director: Jesse Hibbs
Costars: Anne Bancroft, Jay Silverheels,
Charles Drake, Pat Crowley

Murphy plays a factual person in this solid film, Indian agent John Clum, who was known as a principled voice on behalf of the Apache in southern Arizona and the first mayor of Tombstone, AZ. Clum also captured Geronimo without a shot being fired. Filmed in Tucson, Arizona. (The film was originally entitled *Apache Agent* and Murphy later had a racehorse named "Apache Agent" which he himself rode to victory in an owner-trainer race in 1963.)

## THE GUNS OF FORT PETTICOAT
Columbia Pictures
Released April 1957
Technicolor
Director: George Marshall
Costars: Kathryn Grant, Hope Emerson, Ray Teal

Despite a title that hints at the possibilities of light-hearted humor, this film, Murphy's first as an independent producer, fell flat, despite reuniting him with his *Destry* director. Murphy stars as an army officer who deserts his command and trains an outpost of women to fight off an Indian attack. A slow pace and a lackluster script made it a very routine and unremarkable western. Overshadowed two years later by Universal's *Operation Petticoat* starring Cary Grant and Tony Curtis.

## JOE BUTTERFLY
Universal-International
Released July 1957
Technicolor
Director: Jesse Hibbs
Costars: Burgess Meredith and Keenan Wynn

Another forgettable turn and uninspired script, this one an attempted comedy set in postwar Japan. Murphy plays a photographer for an army magazine.

## *NIGHT PASSAGE*

Universal-International
Released August 1957
Technicolor
Director: James Neilson
Costars: Jimmy Stewart, Jack Elam

Audie Murphy turns in an effective portrayal of an outlaw known as "The Utica Kid" who runs with a gang of thieves who have taken to targeting railroad company payrolls. Jimmy Stewart stars as Grant McLaine, hired by the railroad to get the payroll through. The story is complicated by the fact that Stewart's and Murphy's characters are brothers. (That Murphy's character is named "Lee" to Stewart's "Grant" is not the only clichéd element at work, but perhaps the most heavy-handed one.)

Nevertheless, *Night Passage* was the first movie in a long time in which Murphy wasn't the main star—he does not appear until thirty-five minutes into the story. Here he is in a subordinate role to Stewart's lead, and the effective job he does with his part hints at his developing abilities as an actor when he didn't have to carry a film by himself. Filmed partially in Durango, Colorado.

## *SUSPICION*: "THE FLIGHT"

NBC television
Aired November 1957

60 minutes
Black and White
Director: James Neilson
Costars Jack Warden, Everett Sloan, and Susan Kohner, who had
played the role of Maria in *To Hell and Back*

An episode of a series slightly like CBS's *The Twilight Zone* which begin two years later. Murphy plays a former Navy pilot hired to bring back a kidnapped professor from South America. Gene L. Coon, who would go on to write many of the teleplays for the *Star Trek* television series, as well as for Murphy's own very good *No Name on the Bullet*, shared writing credit on this episode.

## *G. E. THEATER*: "INCIDENT"

CBS television
Aired February 1958
30 minutes
Black and White
Hosted by Ronald Reagan
Costars: Darryl Hickman, Robert Patton

Set in the American Civil War, Audie Murphy portrays a Confederate Soldier named Tennessee, while Patton plays a Northern soldier known only as "Yank." The short duration precluded any development or conflict other than that inherent in a Civil War vignette.

## *THE QUIET AMERICAN*

United Artists
Released February 1958

Black and White
Director: Joseph L. Mankiewicz
Costars: Michael Redgrave, Claude Dauphin, Bruce Cabot

Filmed version of Graham Greene's novel in which Audie Murphy plays the title character. A serious and at times subtle movie that deserves much more credit than it widely received, including from Murphy himself, who thought little of the project after it was released. Shot partially in Saigon, Murphy plays the role with his customary restraint. In this case, that restraint coupled with his image of wholesome innocence serves him well. Murphy also captures the naiveté of Graham's character perfectly, especially set against the cool cynicism of Redgrave's character, even as the author criticized Mankiewicz for toning down the anti-American sentiment of the novel. Like the public image of Audie Murphy himself, it's hard to imagine American naiveté and optimism better portrayed. Rewards repeated viewing. Interiors filmed in Rome.

## *RIDE A CROOKED TRAIL*

Universal-International
Released September 1958
Color
Director: Jesse Hibbs
Costars: Walter Matthau, Henry Silva

The pattern in which Audie Murphy follows up a role that stretches his abilities and reputation with a return to simplistic westerns is now well-established. Here, he's back to form playing a bank robber who pretends to be a U.S. marshal and is subsequently forced to become the lawman in a western town.

## THE GUN RUNNERS

United Artists
Released September 1958
Black and White
Director: Don Siegel
Costars: Eddie Albert, Jack Elam, Everett Sloan

A remake of *To Have and Have Not*, with Audie Murphy in the role made famous by Humphrey Bogart. Another attempt to place Murphy in a non-western, this film casts him as a charter boat owner in Key West, Florida who gets pulled into a plot to run guns to Cuba rebels. Murphy was correct in saying it was much like most of his other movies, only with boats instead of horses. Newport Beach and Newport Bay, California stand in for Key West and Cuba.

## NO NAME ON THE BULLET

Universal-International
Released February 1959
Color
Director: Jack Arnold
Costars: Charles Drake, Joan Evans,
Warren Stevens, R. G. Armstrong

One of Audie Murphy's best movies, in which he plays a notorious hired assassin named John Gant who arrives in a quiet western town giving no indication of who his target is. Murphy's low-key and emotionless performance plays perfectly in line with his personality and his character. In few of his movies does he disappear so completely into a part. Numerous lines in which other characters describe Gant could just as easily be describing Murphy himself.

## THE WILD AND THE INNOCENT

Universal-International

Released May 1959

Color

Director: Jack Sher

Costars: Joanne Dru, Jim Backus, Gilbert Roland, Sandra Dee

Forgettable attempt at putting Audie Murphy into a western comedy-romance.

## CAST A LONG SHADOW

United Artists

Released July 1959

Black and White

Director: Thomas Carr

Costars: James Best, Denver Pyle, John Dehner, Terry Moore

Murphy's character inherits a cattle ranch and has to prove himself by leading a trail drive and overcoming assorted villainous rivals.

## FORD STARTIME: "THE MAN"

NBC television

Broadcast January 1960

60 minutes

Color

Director: Robert Stevens

Costars: Joseph Campanella, Thelma Ritter, William Hickey

A live theatrical production broadcast from New York, Murphy gives a solid performance as a paranoid man recently discharged from the army who terrorizes Thelma Ritter's character after she takes him in and gives him a job. Adapted from an original play by Mel Dinelli that had a short run on Broadway in 1950.

## HELL BENT FOR LEATHER
Universal-International
Released February 1960
Color
Director: George Sherman
Costars: Stephen McNally, Felicia Farr

Audie Murphy's character arrives in a small town after his horse is stolen and is mistaken for a murderer. He escapes from the sheriff and sets about proving his innocence.

## THE UNFORGIVEN
United Artists
Released April 1960
Technicolor
Director: John Huston
Costars: Burt Lancaster, Audrey Hepburn, Lillian Gish, Doug McClure

The second teaming of Audie Murphy and John Huston drew an even better performance out of Murphy than did *The Red Badge of Courage*. His role as Cash Zachary is one of his best, if not his very best, and he comes across as completely unselfconscious in a range of emotional intensity absent from his other films. The clearest indication in his entire career of what he could have accomplished given the proper scripts and support. He plays one of three brothers (the other two played by Burt Lancaster and Doug McClure). Filmed in Durango, Mexico.

## SEVEN WAYS FROM SUNDOWN

Universal-International
Released September 1960
Color
Director: Harry Keller, with George Sherman
Costars: Barry Sullivan, John McIntire, Kenneth Tobey, Venetia
Stevenson, Ken Lynch

Back to form. Murphy's character in this movie is actually named "Seven Ways from Sundown Jones" who joins up with the Texas Rangers for typical western action. Filmed in Nevada and Utah.

## POSSE FROM HELL

Universal-International
Released May 1961
Color
Director: Herbert Coleman
Costars: John Saxon, Zohra Lampert, Vic Morrow, Royal Dano,
Lee Van Cleef, Ray Teal

Murphy puts together a posse to pursue the men who killed the local sheriff and kidnapped a girl.

## *WHISPERING SMITH*
NBC television
Made Summer 1959
Aired May–September 1961
30 minutes
Black and White
Director: Various directors
Costars: Guy Mitchell, Sam Buffington

Murphy plays a detective named Tom Smith in this short-lived western television series set in 1870s Denver.

## *BATTLE AT BLOODY BEACH*
20th Century Fox
Released June 1961
Black and White
Director: Herbert Coleman

In Audie Murphy's second war movie, he plays a Navy contractor who is helping to supply irregular forces in the Philippines fighting the Japanese. He is also trying to track down his wife from whom he was separated at the time of the invasion. One critic pointedly noted that outside of the setting there was no difference between this and most of his westerns. Filmed at Catalina Island in California.

## *6 BLACK HORSES*
Universal-International
Released June 1962
Color
Director: Harry Keller

Costars: Dan Duryea, Joan O'Brian, George Wallace

Murphy's cowboy and Duryea's gun slinger (who is saddled with the loaded name of "Frank Jesse") are hired by O'Brian to escort her across Indian territory. The title comes from the six black horses that are typically used to pull a funeral wagon, on which one of the characters finally winds up. Filmed in Utah.

## SHOWDOWN

Universal-International
Released May 1963
Black and White
Director: R. G. Springsteen
Costars: Charles Drake, Strother Martin, L. Q. Jones

In this last movie that Murphy and Drake made together, they play cowboys who are falsely jailed along with a gang of bandits. They all escape together and Murphy's character eventually takes down the gang.

## WAR IS HELL

Allied Artists
Released October 1963
Director: Burt Topper

Murphy supplies only a preface to this war movie, rather like General Walter Bedell Smith provided in *To Hell and Back*, speaking words he knew all too well about what war and fear are like. Despite his limited screen time, it is an impressive turn before the camera and his is the voice of thoughtful authority.

## *GUNFIGHT AT COMANCHE CREEK*
Allied Artists
Released November 1963
Color
Director: Frank McDonald
Costars: Ben Cooper, DeForest Kelley

In perhaps the most unremarkable of Murphy's films, he plays a detective pretending to be an outlaw to trap a gang.

## *THE QUICK GUN*
Columbia Pictures
Released April 1964
Technicolor
Director: Sidney Salkow
Costars: James Best, Merry Anders, Ted de Corsia

Murphy's character is a former outlaw who helps a town fight off his former gang.

## *BULLET FOR A BADMAN*
Universal Pictures
Released October 1964
Color
Director: R. G. Springsteen
Costars: Darren McGavin, Ruta Lee, Alan Hale Jr., Ray Neal

Murphy stars as a former lawman who comes out of retirement to chase down a notorious outlaw who was once married to Murphy's character's wife. Filmed partially in Utah.

# APACHE RIFLES

20th Century Fox
Released November 1964
Color
Director: William Witney
Costars: J. Patrick O'Malley, Ken Lynch,
Michael Dante and L. Q. Jones

A film that stands out, somewhat, from the others Murphy made at this time. Here Murphy's Cavalry Captain Jeff Stanton is the son of an army captain who had been court martialed out of the army for getting his command slaughtered. Determined to erase the shame, Murphy's character has become a determined Indian fighter. Again as in the far more satisfying *Drums Across the River*, Murphy's character gets caught between Indians and settlers and miners who are the threat to stability and peace. Linda Lawson portrays a half-Comanche mission worker who has taken up with the tribe and with whom Murphy's character becomes smitten. Gets a bit preachy on the topic of brotherhood and friendship and perhaps is one of the movies which caused Murphy to want to produce traditional westerns without social commentary.

# ARIZONA RAIDERS

Columbia Pictures
Released August 1965
Technicolor
Director: William Witney
Costars: Michael Dante, Buster Crabbe, Gloria Talbott

Murphy plays a former member of Quantrill's Raiders who gets out of jail and is recruited to infiltrate the remaining gang to bring them to justice. Filmed in Arizona.

## TRUNK TO CAIRO

Noah Films-CCC Film Kunst
Released by American-International, January 1966
Color
Director: Menahem Golan
Costars: George Sanders

Murphy stars in this Israeli-made movie as a James Bond–type secret agent trying to destroy a nuclear missile base near Cairo. Sanders plays the scientist in charge of the installation. Filmed in Israel.

## GUNPOINT

Universal Pictures
Released May 1966
Technicolor
Director: Earl Bellamy
Costars: Joan Staley, Warren Stevens, Denver Pyle,
Royal Dano, Morgan Woodward

Of this movie, Audie Murphy's last for Universal, some of the cast continually joked that it was "a lot of gun and not much point." Murphy is a member of a posse which chases a gang of train robbers into Mexico. It was a cheaply-made movie that recycled a tremendous amount of footage from several of his previous films, including *Night Passage, Sierra, Kansas Raiders*, the *Cimarron Kid*, and all the way back to *Kid from Texas*. Filmed in Utah.

## THE TEXICAN

Columbia Pictures
Released June 1966

Technicolor
Director: Lesley Selander, Jose Luis Espinosa
Costars: Broderick Crawford

Murphy plays a gunfighter who comes out of hiding to track down his brother's killer. Western filmed in Catalonia, Spain, during which time Murphy was severely addicted to sleeping pills.

## 40 GUNS TO APACHE PASS

Columbia Pictures
Released May 1967
Color
Director: William Witney

Audie Murphy's last leading role in a movie finds himself cast as a cavalry captain trying to escort a shipment of repeating rifles to his fort while fending off Indians led by Cochise, and mutinous soldiers ready to turn against him. A solid and at times thoughtful performance.

## A TIME FOR DYING

Fipco Pictures
Released July 1971
Color
Director: Budd Boetticher

In this film, the first produced by his own production company, and his last appearance in the movies, Audie Murphy plays an older Jesse James in a short and rather poignant cameo. Filmed in Arizona.

# NOTES

## INTRODUCTION

1.  Ernie Pyle, quoted in Deborah Solomon, *American Mirror: The Life and Art of Norman Rockwell* (New York: Picador, 2014), 195.
2.  See Jack Valenti, *Ten Heroes and Two Heroines and Other Writings* (Houston: Premier Print Co., 1957), 7.
3.  See Alan Fontana and Robert Rosenheck, "Traumatic War Stressors and Psychiatric Symptoms Among World War II, Korean, and Vietnam War Veterans," *Psychology and Aging* 9, no. 1 (1994), 27–33.
4.  See Max Hastings, "Hollywood Hero," in *Warriors: Extraordinary Tales from the Battlefield* (New York: Vintage, 2007).
5.  Tom Brokaw, *The Greatest Generation* (New York: Random House, 2001), xix.

## CHAPTER 1: A CHILD OF THE DEPRESSION

1.    No account of Audie Murphy's early life would be possible without the work of Harold B. Simpson. His encyclopedic *Audie Murphy: American Soldier*, part biography, part scrapbook, thoroughly chronicles Murphy in a way no other work can hope to do. The vignettes from Murphy's childhood here, along with direct quotations are, unless otherwise noted, largely constructed from this book.

2.    "Wind around a shanty," "poverty dogged," Audie Murphy, *To Hell and Back* (New York: Owl Books, 2002; originally published by Henry Holt and Co., 1949), 75, 6.

3.    See Robert Ozment, "Farming in the Blacklands During the Great Depression," in M. Rebecca Sharpless and Joe C. Yelderman Jr., eds., *The Texas Blackland Prairie: Land, History and Culture* (Waco, TX: Baylor University Press, 1993), 167–76. Farmer quoted on 171.

4.    "Under wing," Don Graham, *No Name on the Bullet: A Biography of Audie Murphy* (New York: Viking, 1989), 13.

5.    "At school," *To Hell and Back*, 7; "mean kid," *Saturday Evening Post*, April 18, 1953, 153.

6.    "Was not lazy," *To Hell and Back*; "never worked a day," *No Name on the Bullet*, 10.

## CHAPTER 2: FINDING A PURPOSE

1.    McClure's comments are in an unpublished manuscript entitled "Helmets in the Dust," in Box 2 of 2, folder 0363, "Manuscript F5 10," Audie Muprhy Papers, Texas Collection, Baylor University.

2.    "A trick stomach," recorded by David McClure, folder 0363, Manuscript F4, Audie Murphy Papers, Texas Collection, Baylor University.

## CHAPTER 3: INTO THE FIGHT

1. "I never felt better," AM to CB, 26 Feb 1943, quoted in Simpson, 198; "There wasn't much to do," in Daniel R. Champagne, *Dogface Soldiers: The Story of B Company, 15th Regiment, 3rd Infantry Division From Fedala to Salzburg: Audie Murphy and his Brothers in Arms* (Bennington, VT: Merriam Press, 2011), 33.

2. "The first time I saw Audie," in "How Audie Won His Medals," by David McClure, manuscript in Folder 0363 Manuscript F4, Box 2 of 2, Audie Murphy Papers, Texas Collection, Baylor University.

3. "I cursed every step," *Dogface Soldiers*, 36.

4. "I hope to see a little action soon," AM to CB, 26 Feb 43, quoted in Simpson, 198.

5. "I learned more," and "Never was any division more fit," *Dogface Soldiers*, 38–39.

6. Ernie Pyle, *Brave Men* (New York: Henry Holt and Co., 1945), 8; "The most gigantic fleet," Rick Atkinson, *The Day of Battle: The War in Sicily and Italy* (New York: Henry Holt and Co., 2007), 33.

7. "The first day at sea," *Brave Men*, 11.

8. Steinbeck in Samuel Hynes, et al., eds., *Reporting World War II: American Journalism 1938–1946* (New York: Library of America, 1995, 2001), 319.

9. "How Audie Won His Medals."

10. *Day of Battle*, 113, 150.

11. *To Hell and Back*, 2–4.

12. Ibid., 11.

13. Ibid., 13, 15.

14. *Dogface Soldiers*, 46–47.

15. Mauldin quoted in *Day of Battle*, 86; "If I discovered one valuable thing," quoted in "How Audie Murphy Won His Medals," Texas Collection, Baylor University.

16. *Brave Men*, 60–63, 20.

17. The remark about not stopping for gas is in *Day of Battle*, 133; "Palermo in five days," quoted in Simpson, 71.

18. *To Hell and Back*, 12.

19. Ibid., 13.

## CHAPTER 4: ITALY

1. Eisenhower quoted in *Day of Battle*, 214.

2. *To Hell and Back*, 15.

3. Martin Blumenson, *United States Army in World War II: The Mediterranean Theater of Operations: Salerno to Cassino* (Washington, DC: Office of the Chief of Military History, U.S. Army, 1969), 194.

4. *To Hell and Back*, 23.

5. "We were like brothers," quoted in *Dogface Soldiers*, 63. In *To Hell and Back*, Audie Murphy calls Tipton "Brandon"; "because it was going to end tomorrow," quoted in *Hero*, 82; Murphy talking of his siblings in the orphanage and "He'd almost come to tears," from an interview with Private Charles Owen, *Audie Murphy Research Foundation newsletter*, vol. 1 (Winter 1997); "The one man who kept me from being afraid," in "Why I Gave My Medals Away," *This Week* magazine, May 29, 1955.

6. His description of Sieja (whom he calls Novak in his book) is in *To Hell and Back*, 19.

7. *To Hell and Back*, 17, 31.

8. Simpson, 91.

9.  Pyle, 97–103; *To Hell and Back*, 34; see Richard Tregaskis in *Reporting WWII*, 323; "better country than this," *Salerno to Cassino*, 235.

10. *To Hell and Back*, 46; *Brave Men*, 58.

11. See *To Hell and Back*, 51–53.

12. "Fugitives from the law of averages," their suspicion and resentment of replacements, and the account of Murphy attacking the replacement who refused to follow orders is in *To Hell and Back*, 109–11.

13. The remarks by John Lucas in this and in subsequent paragraphs, as well as those of Mark Clark below, are in *Salerno to Cassino*, 355–57.

14. See *To Hell and Back*, 80.

15. Ibid., 99.

16. *Brave Men*, 92–93.

17. Ibid., 165.

18. *To Hell and Back*, 84–86, 90–91.

19. This and the following paragraph is from *Dogface Soldiers*, 86–89.

20. "It strikes first," in *To Hell and Back*, 96; "Now there'll be times," in interview with Private Charles Owen, *Audie Murphy Research Foundation newsletter*, vol. 1 (Winter 1997).

21. Simpson, 101–2.

22. *To Hell and Back*, 142.

23. Sevareid quoted in Robert Katz, *The Battle for Rome: The Germans, the Allies, the Partisans, and the Pope* (New York: Simon & Schuster, 2004), 320; "young girls" in *The Battle for Rome*, 318.

24. Ibid., 181.

25. *To Hell and Back*, 163.

26. See "Anecdotes about Audie Murphy," by Colonel Henry R. Bodson, USA (Ret.), http://www.audiemurphy.com/documents/doc049/HenryBodsonRecolletions.pdf.

## CHAPTER 5: A ROAD TO HEROISM

1. For information and analysis of combat fatigue in this and succeeding paragraphs see U.S. Army, *Neuropsychiatry in World War II*, vol. I, especially chapter 14, John W. Appel, "Preventative Psychiatry."

2. One in four, and a million cases, *No Name on the Bullet*, 79.

3. *To Hell and Back*, 170.

4. *Dogface Soldiers*, 123.

5. "Rocky, pine-clad hills," in Samuel Eliot Morison, *History of United States Naval Operations in World War II*, vol. 11, *The Invasion of France and Germany*, 259; quoted in Graham, *No Name on the Bullet*, 90.

6. "I never saw a drop of blood on him," in "How Audie Murphy Won His Medals."

7. *Dogface Soldiers*, 130.

8. *To Hell and Back*, 185–86.

9. *Dogface Soldiers*, 132.

10. These plans and those of the Germans in the following paragraph can be found in Jeffrey J. Clarke and Robert Ross Smith, *United States Army in World War II: The European Theater of Operations: Riviera to the Rhine* (Atlanta, GA: Whitman Publishing, 2012), 171–74; "Champagne campaign," 181.

11. *To Hell and Back*, 195; Telegram quoted in Simpson, 129.

12. Simpson, 129.

13. *To Hell and Back*, 196.

14. Ibid., 203.

15. *Dogface Soldiers*, 149.

16. "born leader and potential officer," quoted in Simpson, 95; "I figured those gentlemen," and "must have had some plan," quoted in *Dogface Soldiers*, 149–50.

17. "I took my time," quoted in *No Name on the Bullet*, 76.

18. *Riviera to the Rhine*, 287.

19. *To Hell and Back*, 217–18; Simpson, 135.

20. "Lord, yes!" quoted in "How Audie Won his Medals"; "Blood and Guts, Jr.," *No Name on the Bullet*, 124.

21. See *Riviera to the Rhine*, 291–92.

22. *Dogface Soldiers*, 154.

## CHAPTER 6: A WEARY VICTOR

1. *To Hell and Back*, 225–26.

2. "The Great American War Hero" quotation is from Carolyn Price, recorded in recollections she wrote down in 1973. The other quotations appear in *No Name on the Bullet*, 83. Much of the material in the next two paragraphs comes from her recollection including her quotations and the story of the two going out in Aix-en-Provence.

3. Carolyn Price recollection of Audie Murphy, Audie Murphy Memorial Website, http://www.audiemurphy.com/documents/doc038/CarolynPriceRyanRecollections_12Feb73.pdf.

4. "a huge and dangerous bridgehead," *To Hell and Back*, 228; "a precarious one," quoted in *The Guns at Last Light*, 480; "Until we get firmly established," in Charles B. Macdonald, *The U.S. Army in World War Two: The Last Offensive* (Washington, DC: Center of Military History, U.S. Army, 1973 reprinted 1993), 55.

5. *Dogface Soldiers*, 176.

6. "Each Alsatian hamlet," in *Riviera to the Rhine*, 486; "toughest assignments in its history," *To Hell and Back*, 228.

7.  *Dogface Soldiers*, 177.

8.  *To Hell and Back*; "in the draws, in the meadows," quoted in *No Name on the Bullet*, 92.

9.  "The whole damn tank destroyer," in *No Name on the Bullet*, 92.

10. "He saved our lives," quoted in *Dogface Soldiers*, 186; "The bravest thing I've ever seen," quoted in *No Name on the Bullet*.

11. *To Hell and Back*, 247.

12. "Courage to spare," in Ibid., 258; "Sleep is not among our rations," in Ibid., 256. For the combat fatigue figures, see *Riviera to the Rhine*, 568.

13. "I have seen too much," and "Why not mine?" in *To Hell and Back*, 263; "almost fatalistic view," *No Name on the Bullet*, 95.

14. "Relative safety," in Anecdotes about Audie Murphy, Colonel Henry R. Bodson, USA (Ret.), Audie Murphy Memorial Website.

15. *To Hell and Back*, 265–68.

16. "Like a great river," in Ibid., 268; "We are moving so fast," and the story of him letting the German soldiers who were "gabbing, horsing around, eating their rations," are in *No Name on the Bullet*, 97.

17. Quoted in *Dogface Soldiers*, 233.

## CHAPTER 7: A HERO RETURNS TO TEXAS

1.  His time at the hotel in Cannes is related in *To Hell and Back*, 272–73.

2.  See unpublished manuscript by AM entitled "Helmets in the Dust," in BOX 2 of 2, folder 0363 "Manuscript F5 10," Audie Murphy Papers, Texas Collection, Baylor University.

3.  Bodson, "Anecdotes about Audie Murphy."

4.  The details and quotations from this episode are from Price's recollection of Audie Murphy, http://www.audiemurphy.com/documents/doc038/CarolynPriceRyanRecollections_12Feb73.pdf.

5.    See Simpson, 233.

6.    Don Graham points out that the banquet was the first time some-
      one publically described Murphy as winning "every medal in the
      book." *No Name*, 105; the story of him seducing the elevator girl
      is in *No Name on the Bullet*, 104–5, and in Whiting, *Hero*.

7.    "I just fought to stay alive," in Lois Sager Foxhall, "Audie Murphy:
      A Recollection," *Dallas Morning News*, June 6, 1971.

8.    "Celeste Awaits Return Lt. Murphy," Greenville *Morning Herald*,
      July 11, 1945.

9.    "When Murphy Comes Home Farmersville to Celebrate," Green-
      ville *Morning Herald*, June 8, 1945.

10.   See "Audie is Home," *Saturday Evening Post*, September 15, 1945.

11.   "I'm not sure," in Foxhall, "Audie Murphy," *Dallas Morning
      News*, June 6, 1971.

12.   "Texas' Top Hero Blushes as 5000 Pay Him Tribute," *Waco News
      Tribune*, June 16, 1945.

13.   See "Lt. Audie Murphy Visits Wounded," *Ft. Worth Star-Tele-
      gram*, June 20, 1945.

## CHAPTER 8: A HERO GOES TO HOLLYWOOD

1.    Doug Warren with James Cagney, *James Cagney: The Authorized
      Biography* (New York: St. Martin's Press, 1983), 162.

2.    "When I met him at the plane," quoted in *No Name on the Bullet*,
      129.

3.    Quoted in Simpson, 257.

4.    "Real Hero to Reel Hero," *Houston Chronicle*, February 15, 1947;
      "Publicity gimmicks" quoted in *No Name on the Bullet*, 130.

5.    The curriculum is outlined in Mel Gordon, *Stanislavsky in Amer-
      ica: An Actor's Workbook* (London and New York: Routledge,

2010), 117; "hayshaker," James Cagney, 162; "Not standard speech," *No Name on the Bullet*, 137.

6.    See Don Graham in *No Name on the Bullet*, 135; "A burlesque queen's garters," in *Stanislavsky in America*, 119; "Leftists and Commie lovers," quoted in *The Films of Audie Murphy*, 22; "Even I could see," *No Name on the Bullet*, 135.

7.    For the petition see *Variety*, October 28, 1947.

8.    See Jules Tygiel, *Ronald Reagan and the Triumph of American Conservatism* (New York: Pearson Longman, 2006), 59.

9.    For his speech at the Beverly Hills AVC meeting, see *Variety*, April 17, 1946; "One of the most left-leaning of the variety of groups," quoted in Tygiel, *Ronald Reagan*, 58; for "The Case of the Missing Homes," see *Variety*, January 16, 1947.

10.   See *Variety*, May 29, 1946; "A challenge to the liberties," quoted in *No Name on the Bullet*, 136.

11.   "I can't even make a living," quoted in *No Name on the Bullet*, 137.

12.   "If it hadn't been for Wanda," quoted in Ibid., 168.

13.   "Add Roma Bohnen to Remarque Film," *The Brooklyn Daily Eagle*, August 24, 1946, 12; "Two Soldiers," in *Variety*, Friday, Nov. 29, 1946, 2.

14.   See *No Name on the Bullet*, 143–44; the *New York Times* took note of the story as well, but reported that the hitchhiker attempted to rob Murphy at a rural gas station. See "Little War Hero Fells Goliath," *New York Times*, December 15, 1946.

15.   Farrow and Murphy both quoted in *The Films of Audie Murphy*, 22–23.

16.   See "Hedda Hopper, Columnist, Dies; Chronicled Gossip of Hollywood," *New York Times*, February 2, 1966.

17.   "It turned out," *James Cagney*, 162.

18.   "Shower and steam bath," quoted in Simpson, 261

19. "Nimitz with Heroes," *Austin American Statesman*, October 16, 1947.

20. "Prattling nonsense," quoted in *No Name on the Bullet*, 170; See *Life* magazine, November 17, 1949, 106–11; "I don't think it's very serious," quoted in "Texas Hero Will Marry Film Beauty," *Austin Statesman*, July 20, 1948.

21. "I would have killed him," *No Name on the Bullet*, 171; "such deadly menace," "Just for Variety," *Variety*, November 3, 1947, 4.

22. "writing in a school composition book," *Saturday Evening Post*, April 18, 1953, 155; "Just for Variety," *Variety*, March 17, 1948, 4.

23. "Influenced Spec for the better," and "For a Young Man's Heart," in *No Name on the Bullet*, 156, 157.

24. There is a copy of these early pages of Murphy's memoir in the Audie Murphy Papers, Box 2 of 2, folder 0363 "Manuscript F5 10," Audie Murphy Papers, Texas Collection, Baylor University.

25. Bob Larkins and Boyd Magers, *The Films of Audie Murphy* (Jefferson, NC: McFarland & Co., Publishers, 2004), 29.

26. "Hackneyed, insipid and illogical," *New York Times*, March 23, 1949; "Washington Hullabaloo," *Variety*, September 22, 1948, 6.

## CHAPTER 9: THE MAKING OF A STAR

1. Audie Murphy, "The Role I Liked Best...," *Saturday Evening Post*, January 13, 1951, 113.

2. Charles Poore, "Books of the Times," *New York Times*, March 10, 1949.

3. The episode is recorded in *No Name on the Bullet*, 183; See also "Audie Murphy is Giving his 24 Medals to Children," *New York Times*, June 9, 1950.

4.  "Audie Murphy Gives All His War Medals Away," *Austin States-man*, June 8, 1950.

5.  Arness quoted in *The Films of Audie Murphy*, 37.

6.  "Fighting harder," quoted in *The Films of Audie Murphy*, 38; "let 'em scream," *Variety*, September 1, 1949, 4.

7.  "Audie is not well," quoted in *The Films of Audie Murphy*, 40; "a lamb around a grizzly," quoted in *No Name on the Bullet*, 174.

8.  "Actresses, not war veterans," quoted in *No Name on the Bullet*, 185–86.

9.  Quoted in Ibid., 190.

10. See "Wanda Hendrix Asks Divorce," *New York Times*, February 18, 1950.

11. David McClure, BOX 2 of 2, folder 0363 "Manuscript F5 10," ms page 6, Audie Murphy Papers, Texas Collection, Baylor University.

12. "With so many," quoted in *No Name on the Bullet*, 197.

13. Quoted in *Films of Audie Murphy*, 43.

14. "They'd rather have a star," quoted in Lillian Ross, *Picture*, 16.

15. "A damn fool idea," quoted in "Two Youthful Vets Star in Battle Film," *Austin Statesman*, August 16, 1950; "Happiest and most appropriate casting," and "For a change," quoted in *Picture*, 34.

16. "Everything John Huston suggested," and "Audie is afraid of making a fool," both in *The Films of Audie Murphy*, 48, 149.

17. *Picture*, 21.

18. Reinhardt quoted in Ibid., 76.

19. Ibid., 36.

20. Ibid., 16.

21. Easton and Dano quoted in *The Films of Audie Murphy*, 47, 53.

22. Mauldin's comments in this and in the subsequent paragraph come from "Parting Shots," *Life* Magazine, June 11, 1971.

23. *No Name on the Bullet*, 170.

24. "A Round-Up of Western Badmen," *New York Times*, January 26, 1951.

25. *Films*, 47.

26. Quoted in *No Name on the Bullet*, 194.

27. "Audie Murphy Joins 36th," *Austin Statesman*, July 14, 1950.

28. "Audie Murphy Sees New GIs Better Men," *Austin Statesman*, June 18, 1951; "Audie Murphy Ends Duty Tour," *Austin Statesman*, September 30, 1951.

29. *No Name on the Bullet*, 213, 235.

30. Conspicuous by its absence," *Films of Audie Murphy*, 55; "Sure I like making Westerns," quoted in *No Name on the Bullet*, 222.

## CHAPTER 10: TO HELL AND BACK

1. "It is very difficult," quoted in *No Name on the Bullet*, 233; "Audie Murphy Denies He Is Quitting Pictures," *Austin Statesman*, October 10, 1950.

2. See "Lamour, Autry, Audie in Dallas," *Variety*, May 20, 1953.

3. McFadden's recollections are in *No Name on the Bullet*, 225–28.

4. "I don't have a father," quoted in Ibid., 228.

5. "Sure-shot guy," *No Name on the Bullet*, 230; "18 day shooting schedule," *Films of Audie Murphy*, 83; Reagan quoted in "Actor, Governor, President, Icon," *Washington Post*, June 6, 2004.

6. "Audie was a gambler who wouldn't cheat," *Films of Audie Murphy*, 115; "Always unlucky," *No Name on the Bullet*, 256.

7. Elam quoted in *Films*, 115. "$200,000 on a horse," *No Name on the Bullet*, 257.

8. "Just for Variety," *Variety*, November 13, 1951.

9. "Dullest town," Thomas B. Morgan, "The War Hero," *Esquire*, December 1983, 602; McClure quoted in *Hero*, 210; For Murphy

continuing to chase women after his marriage, see *No Name on the Bullet*, 279–81.

10.  Murphy's comments here and in the next paragraph are from "Audie Murphy: Hunting Proved Valuable in War," *Dallas Morning News*, September 16, 1962.

11.  "I'm too impulsive," *No Name on the Bullet*, 236.

12.  See Ibid., 278–79; "It's About Time," *Houston Chronicle*, June 12, 1988; "Murphy Has Role in Arrest," *Dallas Morning News*, April 25, 1956, 1; "To keep from being bored to death," quoted in Thomas B. Morgan "The War Hero," *Esquire*, December, 1983.

13.  "Jesse Hibbs to Meg Audie's Autobiopic," *Variety*, December 29, 1953.

14.  "Lousy book," quoted in "He Doesn't Want to be a Star," *Saturday Evening Post*, April 18, 1953, 240.

15.  Quoted in *No Name on the Bullet*, 241.

16.  "hate, frustration, horror," quoted in Ibid., 242.

17.  "tenacious about every point," quoted in *Films of Audie Murphy*, 93; "No Hollywood hero," *Life* magazine, July 4, 1955, 67; "to see done right," Herbert Mitgang, "War is 'To Hell and Back' for Audie Murphy," *New York Times*, September 25, 1955.

18.  "To Hell and Back," *New York Times*, September 23, 1955.

19.  See *Hero*, 221.

20.  See "UI to Hoopla 'Hell' On TV With Nat'l Spot Splurge," *Variety*, June 21, 1955.

21.  "No Hollywood Hero," *Life* magazine, July 4, 1955, 67–70.

22.  "'To Hell and Back' Surprise Record-Breaker in Openings," *Dallas Morning News*, August 22, 1955, 10.

23.  "Audie Murphy Tells Senate," *Variety*, July 15, 1955.

24.  "Bona Fide Stardom Of Lad Called Audie," *Dallas Morning News*, August 27, 1955.

25. "'Hell & Back' Sock 17G On 1st Day in L.A.," *Variety*, October 14, 1955; for talk of *The Way Back*, see *Variety*, April 9, 1956. For Murphy buying the rights from U-I, see *Variety*, June 26, 1957 and September 24, 1959.

26. "Audie Murphy Sells Farm," *Dallas Morning News*, July 14, 1956, 3.

27. *Films of Audie Murphy*, 99.

28. "Audie to Star Self in Publicist's Story," *Variety*, September 30, 1955.

29. *Variety*, November 24, 1958; and *No Name on the Bullet*, 265.

30. *Variety*, August 9, 1957; October 1, 1958; June 27, 1955; and July 20, 1955.

31. "Audie shouldn't have been playing comedy," quoted in *Films of Audie Murphy*, 109.

32. His illness was mentioned in *Variety* at least twice. See *Variety*, December 13, 1955; and June 14, 1956.

33. "Perfect symbol of what I want to say," "Producer Finds 'Quiet American,'" *New York Times*, December 14, 1956.

34. "I'd be doing myself a favor," *Variety*, January 14, 1957; "No Rest for the 'Quiet American,'" *New York Times*, April 28, 1957.

35. "The commies were only 16 miles," quoted in "Texas Audie Making 29th Western," *Dallas Morning News*, November 27, 1963.

36. See "Screen: 'Quiet American,'" *New York Times*, February 6, 1958; *Variety*, January 22, 1958; Merlin and Murphy quoted in *Films of Audie Murphy*, 123, 121.

37. "Audie Murphy and 13 Days," *Dallas Morning News*, December 13, 1958, 9.

38. See *Variety*, June 20, 1956 and October 31, 1956.

## CHAPTER 11: RIDING A CROOKED TRAIL

1.  Jay Fishburn quoted in *Audie Murphy Research Foundation Newsletter*, vol. 2 (Spring, 1997).

2.  *Films of Audie Murphy*, 126, 116.

3.  Siegel's comments are included in the Turner Classic Movies archive of film commentary, online at http://www.tcm.com/this-month/article/297136%7C0/The-Gun-Runners.html.

4.  "Gentle Audie Blows His Lid," *Dallas Morning News*, December 9, 1958; *Films of Audie Murphy*, 130.

5.  "Audie Murphy played a very good Audie Murphy," quoted in *No Name on the Bullet*, 274; Armstrong's comment about inner reality is in *Films of Audie Murphy*, 133.

6.  "Unique Gift," *Dallas Morning News*, December 23, 1958, 7.

7.  *Films of Audie Murphy*, 140.

8.  See *Variety*, December 19, 1958; "oil and water," in *No Name on the Bullet*, 281.

9.  See "TV Review: Psychological Murder Drama, on *Startime*," *New York Times*, January 6, 1960.

10. "Audie Murphy Stars in War Film Here," *New York Times*, August 17, 1961.

11. "Audie Murphy is back with his old outfit," *Stars and Stripes*, June 24, 1960.

12. *Variety*, February 1, 1961.

13. "Whose Side is He On?" *Variety Weekly*, June 14, 1961; "T.V. Probe Moves to N.Y.," *Variety Weekly*, June 14, 1961.

14. "Texas Audie Making 29th Western," *Dallas Morning News*, November 27, 1963.

## CHAPTER 12: NO NAME ON THE BULLET

1.   Dedication Address at the Alabama War Memorial Ceremony, Decatur, Alabama, July 20, 1968, http://www.audiemurphy.com/documents/doc031/07-20-68_awm.pdf.

2.   "Audie Murphy: Hunting Proved Valuable in War," *Dallas Morning News*, September 16, 1962.

3.   Norman Jewison quoted in "Location-Shooting Learns America Wipes Out All 'Landmarks,'" *Weekly Variety*, November 26, 1969.

4.   "Age is the worst thing of all," in *No Name on the Bullet*, 229.

5.   Staley in *Films of Audie Murphy*, 203.

6.   *TV Guide*, July 29–Aug 4, 1961; Staley in *Films of Audie Murphy*, 203.

7.   Staley in *Films of Audie Murphy*, 203; Whiting, *Hero*, 181.

8.   *Weekly Variety*, January 11, 1967; "worst James Bond parody," *Films of Audie Murphy*, 214.

9.   See critic Bret Wood's assessment of *The Texican* online at http://www.tcm.com/ tcmdb/title/16454/The-Texican/articles.html#00.

10.   For the struggle to break his addiction in this and the following paragraphs, see Thomas B. Morgan, "The War Hero," *Esquire*, December, 1983.

11.   "Was leading a life that was drifting," in *No Name on the Bullet*, 277; "Never admit," in Ibid., 318; the following account of Murphy's gambling and interaction with organized crime is from 321–24.

12.   "It's About Time," *Houston Chronicle*, June 12, 1988.

13.   "Exploited by half the hack producers," quoted in "Texas Audie Murphy Sets Dallas Premier," *Dallas Morning News*, August 25, 1969; "Milk it dry," quoted in *No Name on the Bullet*, 296.

14. "I'm too tough," quoted in "Texas Audie Murphy Sets Dallas Premier," *Dallas Morning News*, August 25, 1969.

15. "I didn't care for," *Films of Audie Murphy*, 218.

16. "Audie Murphy Re-Teams With Budd Boetticher; 'Dying' for Arizona," *Weekly Variety*, April 23, 1969; "He didn't think much," quoted in *No Name on the Bullet*, 311.

17. "Murphy, Boetticher Will Film 'A Horse,'" *Variety*, May 26, 1969; "Boetticher, Murphy Team For 2D Oater," *Weekly Variety*, June 25, 1969. See also "Western Cycle Rolls Again, Black Angle Boosts Take," *Weekly Variety*, June 25, 1969.

18. "Audie Never Yelled for Help Before, But He Sure Could Use It," *Houston Chronicle*, September 15, 1968.

19. "Audie Sued for 15½ G," *Variety*, October 31, 1969; Whiting, *Hero*, 207; *Films*, 218.

20. *Variety* covered the dismal affair from start to finish in a superficial kind of way. See *No Name on the Bullet*, 313–18, for a good account.

21. *Variety*, August 20, 1970.

22. "Audie Murphy to Host War Hero Radio Series," *Weekly Variety*, May 29, 1968. He had completed all 260 narrations when he was killed, after which the program was shelved. See *Weekly Variety*, June 16, 1971.

23. "Murphy Had Extra Points but No Home to Go To," *Montgomery Journal-Advertiser*, July 21, 1968; "Hate their guts," *Esquire*, December 1983, 604.

24. "Opposition to Calley's Conviction and Sentence Grows in Nation," *New York Times*, April 2, 1971.

25. *Variety*, June 2, 1971.

26. See "Bodies Recovered," *Dallas Morning News*, June 1, 1971. A year later the National Transportation Safety Board blamed the pilot in the accident, reporting that he lacked the skill to fly in bad

weather and experience flying in the kind of terrain around Roanoke, Virginia. See "Plane Crash Blamed on Weak Pilot," *Dallas Morning News*, June 15, 1972.

27. See "Audie Murphy Called 'Courageous Warrior'," *Dallas Morning News*, June 5, 1971; also Simpson, 389–93.

28. "I never knew," in "Audie Murphy Buried With Full Honors," *Dallas Morning News*, June 8, 1971; also Simpson, 393–94; Roy Edwards, "Of a Different Time," *Dallas Morning News*, June 2, 1971.

29. "'To Hell and Back' Gives Key to Murphy Heroism," *Dallas Morning News*, August 21, 1955, 1.

# INDEX

# G

# H

# Y

# Z